RAND EDUCATION

Raising the Bar

Louisiana's Strategies for Improving Student Outcomes

Julia H. Kaufman, Jill S. Cannon, Shelly Culbertson, Margaret Hannan, Laura S. Hamilton, Sophie Meyers

Sponsored by the Baton Rouge Area Foundation

For more information on this publication, visit www.rand.org/t/RR2303

Library of Congress Cataloging-in-Publication Data is available for this publication.
ISBN: 978-1-9774-0065-9

Published by the RAND Corporation, Santa Monica, Calif.

© Copyright 2018 RAND Corporation

RAND® is a registered trademark.

Cover: caption/source information.

Support RAND
Make a tax-deductible charitable contribution at
www.rand.org/giving/contribute

www.rand.org

Preface

This report provides an in-depth description of Louisiana's approach to improving educational experiences and student outcomes. Louisiana has received recent attention for some of its new policies and promising early results. Thus, its approaches could merit closer study. As we document, Louisiana's most recent reforms have focused not only on K–12 academics but also on the systems that coexist and interact with K–12 academics, including teacher preparation, early childhood education, and graduation pathways. We particularly focus on the reform strategies that the Louisiana Department of Education (LDOE) has been implementing since 2012, when a new state superintendent of schools was appointed by the Louisiana Board of Elementary and Secondary Education. Since that time, LDOE has utilized a range of policy levers to work toward its goals. These policy levers include accountability but also emphasize resources, tools, and incentives intended to support and build capacity for accountability mandates. What is perhaps most notable about Louisiana's approach is the systematic, focused, and frequent communication and planning processes LDOE has set in motion to support its reform efforts.

This overview of Louisiana's education reform strategies should be of interest to those seeking to keep track of the vast changes being made in the state, as well as education stakeholders in other states who are interested in making system-wide changes to affect educational outcomes. However, we have not yet collected any data on how Louisiana's strategies are being perceived and implemented by stakeholders at the ground level, such as teachers, school leaders, and child care agencies. In addition, we have not investigated how these policy strategies might be linked to improvements in student outcomes over time. We expect to collect such data over the course of 2018 and to publish a report on what we learn, sometime in 2019.

Given that this report focuses only on Louisiana's strategies for improving education, we do not provide any recommendations to consider going forward. Instead, we provide a summary of Louisiana's key actions and the policy levers represented by those actions, which other states can reflect on and consider. We also discuss a number of potential implementation challenges, based on our own reflection and interviews with LDOE staff. We plan to explore these implementation challenges in our continuing research over the next year.

This research was sponsored by the Baton Rouge Area Foundation and conducted within RAND Education, a division of RAND Corporation. For more about RAND Education, visit www.rand.org/education.

Contents

Figures and Tables

Figures

Tables

Summary

Over the past few decades, in response to the No Child Left Behind Act Act of 2001 (NCLB) and the Race to the Top (RTTT) initiative of 2009, states across the United States have passed an unprecedented amount of legislation aimed at making schools and teachers more accountable for student learning. Although the federal legislation has provided states with broad parameters to guide their respective accountability plans, the specific legislative and policy choices that states have made in response to NCLB and RTTT have differed dramatically from state to state, potentially driven to some extent by variations in available federal and state funding. Different states use different tests and very different systems for evaluating student achievement and progress, as well as for determining what counts (and how to calculate what counts) in teacher and school evaluations. To date, no research has taken a holistic look at how individual states have understood and responded to federal accountability legislation within the context of their state-specific priorities to support better outcomes for students.

This report is an attempt to track education reform efforts in the wake of NCLB and RTTT in a single state: Louisiana. Few other states have experienced as much political and social turbulence in their education systems over the past several years as Louisiana. Even before Hurricane Katrina wrought costly devastation in Louisiana in 2005, Louisiana was (and remains) one of the poorest states in the nation (Bishaw and Benson, 2017). Low kindergarten readiness rates, national assessment scores, and college attainment, as well as high unemployment rates among high school graduates, have defined the Louisiana education system for decades. Since 2012, however, state education leaders have enacted a large set of system-wide reforms to improve education quality and outcomes across the state.

Some of Louisiana's reforms have been extensive in scope—for example, restructuring the early childhood education (ECE) system—while others, such as mathematics curriculum reforms, have been structurally modest. Early evidence suggests that these reform efforts may be having a positive effect on outcomes: For example, state scores on the ACT have improved, and Advanced Placement (AP) course completions, high school graduation numbers, and college enrollment rates have risen. A RAND report also documented that teachers in Louisiana are thinking and teaching in ways that are more aligned with their state standards than teachers in other states (Kaufman, Thompson, and Opfer, 2016).

What reforms and actions may be helping to improve education outcomes in Louisiana? To answer this question, researchers from the RAND Corporation tracked how Louisiana has used particular policy levers: specific mandates, resource alignment, incentives, and communication and planning processes. These levers have been "pulled" to address challenges in four major areas: ECE, kindergarten through 12th grade (K–12) academics, K–12 teacher preparation, and graduation pathways. Figure S.1 summarizes the Louisiana Department of Education's (LDOE's) intended theory of implementation. While not every piece of LDOE's work fits perfectly with this cycle, aspects of this theory appear in multiple areas of the reform efforts that we have tracked for this investigation. This theory of implementation relies particularly heavily on communication as a policy lever to improve outcomes for students.

Whether these processes are working exactly as intended to support policy implementation has yet to be determined. Future reports published as part of our overall study will consider how Louisiana policies are being translated by key stakeholders, as well as how state actions are leading to changes in stakeholder behaviors and student outcomes. The present report has three main purposes: (1) to track Louisiana's reform efforts and early signs of the potential success of these efforts, (2) to set the stage for more in-depth analyses of state policy implementation and student outcomes that might be linked to Louisiana's

Figure S.1
Louisiana Department of Education's Theory of Implementation

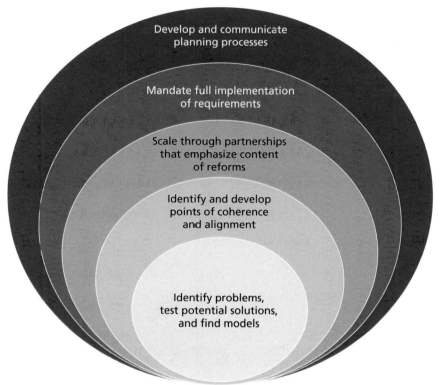

Develop and communicate
planning processes

Mandate full implementation
of requirements

Scale through partnerships
that emphasize content
of reforms

Identify and develop
points of coherence
and alignment

Identify problems,
test potential solutions,
and find models

reform efforts, and (3) to take stock of the differences among the strategies and levers that Louisiana has relied on to reform various areas of its education system. This third purpose, in particular, may have implications for research on how policies can best support innovation and educational improvement.

To document the state's numerous reform efforts and strategies, we brought together multiple data sources, including interviews with 24 state officials; state policy documentation; observations of a professional development convening for Louisiana teachers and school leaders held in September 2017; and Kaufman, Thompson, and Opfer's

(2016) earlier work on Louisiana's educational policy, teachers' knowledge of state standards, and classroom practices.

This overview of Louisiana's strategies to improve student outcomes should be of interest not only to education stakeholders in the state (legislators, state partners, education organizations and institutions, districts and schools, etc.) but also those in other states who are interested in making system-wide changes to improve educational outcomes. It should be noted that this report is only the first in a series; while this report documents key education goals and actions in Louisiana, later work will examine whether and how specific actions are working to bring about desired outcomes. Rather than offering recommendations to consider going forward, we identify a number of themes that could be connected with change and improvement in all areas of Louisiana's education reforms. These themes can be considered by other states looking to make changes across their respective education systems. We provide a more detailed summary of Louisiana's strategies, key actions, and potential implementation challenges in each area that is a focus of this report.

Early Childhood Education: State Strategies and Potential Challenges

Over the past several years, Louisiana has engaged in a series of reforms to address challenges specific to its ECE system. Unequal access to high-quality programs, variations in quality across the state's approximately 1,500 publicly funded ECE programs, and a lack of information to guide parents when choosing programs all likely have contributed to consistent underperformance among children on kindergarten literacy assessments, as measured since 2012.

Key State Strategies
In partnership with the Governor's Office and the Board of Elementary and Secondary Education (BESE), LDOE has set out to foster a common understanding of what ECE program quality looks like, and LDOE has refined that vision through piloting efforts and community

input. The state is supporting the movement toward consistent, high-quality ECE programs with a set of mandates combined with aligned resources and incentives to facilitate program quality improvement, measurement, and access. Integral to this approach is the communication with and involvement of key partners, such as ECE community networks, during the planning and implementation phases; also integral is the creation of structures to enable and support this communication. These reform efforts have redefined and unified the ECE system, and they have also created a shared vision of high-quality early learning focused on improving kindergarten readiness for Louisiana's students from birth to age five.

The foundational legislation related to recent ECE system reforms was the Early Childhood Care and Education Act (also known as "Act 3") of 2012. Act 3, a joint effort by the Governor's Office and LDOE to better prepare children for kindergarten, sought to unify a complex and fragmented system of early childhood programs in the state by shifting governance and accountability for publicly funded programs serving children from birth to age five under a single umbrella through the Louisiana BESE. Act 3 and subsequent legislation also mandated that the LDOE and BESE create an assessment and accountability system for programs, as well as a system of local ECE networks that provide coordinated enrollment across programs to provide access to high-quality ECE centers. To further unify the system, legislation passed in 2014 moved all ECE center licensing under LDOE, shifting Head Start and state child care program licensing functions over from the Department of Children and Family Services (DCFS).

Policy-Related Early Childhood Education Actions

While Act 3 established a broad vision and began to unify the complex system, the state engaged in six key actions to support its vision. These actions drew on a range of policy levers, including mandates, aligned resources, incentives, and communication and planning processes. Table S.1 summarizes the actions, policy levers, and early progress made in meeting outcomes.

Table S.1
Early Childhood Education Actions in Louisiana

Action	Policy Lever	Early Progress
1. Create and require a unified rating system, connected to licensure and funding for all publicly funded centers, to provide information on center quality.	Mandate	• LDOE provides publicly available, annual ratings for all publicly funded centers.
2. Strengthen lead teacher preparation requirements through a new ECE teacher credential: the Early Childhood Ancillary Certificate.	Mandate	• Starting in 2019, lead teachers in publicly funded centers will be required to have an Early Childhood Ancillary Certificate. • 14 Early Childhood Ancillary Certificate programs have been approved by BESE as of January 2018.
3. Signal to ECE staff which curricula, formative assessments, and professional development are high-quality and standards-aligned.	Resource alignment	• Numerous ECE curriculum reviews have been completed and made available online. • LDOE also recommends and supports use of Teaching Strategies GOLD for curriculum-aligned assessments. • Use of curriculum and assessment are publicly reported to families.
4. Increase funding for Child Care Assistance Program (CCAP) subsidies to increase parity, and encourage diversity in types of centers serving publicly funded children.	Incentive	• BESE increased subsidy rates and loosened the eligibility requirements for subsidies to provide greater access. • Louisiana used existing funding through the Nonpublic Schools Early Childhood Development Program and secured new funding through the federal Preschool Expansion Grant program to provide additional pre-kindergarten slots in child care settings.
5. Provide funding incentives tied to higher quality ratings, teacher training, and curriculum use.	Incentive	• Louisiana provides tax credits and bonuses to centers with higher ratings and teachers with certification who stay in the ECE field. • Louisiana provides tuition scholarships for teachers pursuing their Early Childhood Ancillary Certificate and funding to those starting Early Childhood Ancillary Certificate programs. • LDOE reimburses centers for 80 percent of cost of highly rated curricula.

Table S.1—continued

Action	Policy Lever	Early Progress
6. Define and require community networks for administration and communication, including coordinated ECE program enrollment for families.	Communication and planning processes	• 65 lead network agencies plan and coordinate network administrative functions, classroom observations, and coordinated enrollment. • LDOE provides ongoing technical assistance and tools such as guidebooks to support planning processes for lead agencies and ECE centers.

Potential Challenges Related to Early Childhood Education Actions

Louisiana has undertaken rapid changes in ECE policies over the past several years, but challenges remain in meeting Act 3 goals and related actions. Potential challenges include (1) ensuring that families have reliable and accessible information on center quality ratings with which to make better informed child care decisions, as well as that families have equitable access to centers; (2) achieving statewide consensus on the value of ECE center ratings; (3) supporting the Early Childhood Ancillary Certificate system for all teachers; and (4) ensuring that centers are adopting and successfully implementing curricula that have been reviewed as high-quality. We will examine the extent to which these challenges are present in our upcoming research in Louisiana over the next year, and also the extent to which they are obstacles to supporting and improving ECE for children in Louisiana.

K–12 Academics and Teacher Preparation: State Strategies and Potential Challenges

Louisiana students frequently score at lower levels than their peers on various measures of student success, although they have made some progress in recent years. Some of Louisiana's strategies for improving K–12 academics are similar to those strategies targeting curricula and formative assessments in ECE. In addition, to address potential misalignment between teacher preparation and what is emphasized in

K–12 schools, Louisiana has made considerable reforms to policies for teacher preparation.

Key K–12 Academics and Teacher Preparation Strategies

Curricula play a central role in LDOE's strategies to support high-quality teaching and learning. LDOE has used standards and assessments in key content areas to define quality, and it has paid particular attention to providing schools with resources and tools closely aligned with those standards and assessments. In addition, LDOE has been mindful to involve and partner with educators and other stakeholders across the state. For example, LDOE has involved both publishers and districts in the development of curriculum review policies and piloting of curricula, and it has enlisted teacher leader advisers from across the state to perform curriculum reviews. LDOE has also worked with vendors and experts to develop and/or recommend both formative assessments and professional development opportunities that closely align with high-quality curricula.

In the area of K–12 teacher preparation, in particular, LDOE's work began with information-gathering to understand teacher, district, and preparation program needs, and LDOE communicated these findings through reports and community meetings. LDOE then provided funding for districts to partner with teacher preparation organizations and "test out" competencies and yearlong residencies. This work established buy-in that provided more support for mandated requirements, which were passed into policy by the Louisiana Board of Elementary and Secondary Education in 2016.

Policy-Related K–12 System and Teacher Preparation Actions

To meet the goals addressed by state standards in core content areas, LDOE has engaged in seven actions that support educators in schools and classrooms, as well as those who are preparing to be educators. The actions, policy levers, and early progress are documented in Table S.2.

Table S.2
K–12 System and Teacher Preparation Actions in Louisiana

Action	Policy Lever	Early Progress
1. Use state standards, assessments, and accountability to define and communicate a high bar for what is expected from schools and students.	Mandate: Every Student Succeeds Act (ESSA)	• LDOE staff has ensured that the state assessments remained well aligned with standards. • Public reporting from the state comes in the form of school and district report cards, as well as reports to parents.
2. Codify a vision for high-quality teacher preparation that includes clear requirements and accountability structures for teacher preparation programs.	Mandate	• BESE passed teacher preparation requirements for competency-based coursework and yearlong residencies in 2016, with a quality rating system for teacher preparation programs passed into policy in 2017. • Prior to requirements going into policy, LDOE provided support for district-teacher preparation program partnerships to implement the requirements.
3. Signal to educators which instructional materials—including curricula and assessments—are high-quality and which are not.	Resource alignment	• LDOE partnered with educators to provide online reviews regarding which curricula and formative assessments are high-quality and which are not. • LDOE also provides banks of formative assessment items aligned with curricula that have been rated as high-quality.
4. Increase the supply of high-quality, curriculum-specific professional development options, and provide clear information about those options.	Resource alignment	• LDOE provides a catalog of vendors offering professional development resources aligned with specific curricula and assessments that have been rated as high-quality. • Louisiana also provides regional and statewide professional development options closely aligned with high-quality curricula.
5. Provide funding incentives tied to use of high-quality curricula, professional development, and formative assessments.	Incentive	• Louisiana supports district procurement of high-quality curricula with state contracts. • LDOE also provides open access to formative assessments strongly aligned with Tier I curricula. • Most recently, districts must demonstrate they use a high-quality curriculum to receive competitive grant funding.

Table S.2—continued

Action	Policy Lever	Early Progress
6. Incentivize early adoption of the state's vision for high-quality teacher preparation through district-teacher preparation program partnership funding.	Incentive	• LDOE has funded several cohorts district-teacher preparation partnerships since 2014. • By 2017, about 80 percent of Louisiana districts had received funding to support district-teacher preparation partnerships, including stipends for residents and mentors.
7. Create communication structures to identify champions and gather information.	Communication and planning processes	• LDOE has identified key communication structures to reach out to individuals at every layer of the education system, including teachers, principals, superintendents, and many others. • LDOE has identified specific educators across the state who communicate about state policies and share their expertise with others. • Louisiana has partnered with schools, teacher preparation programs, and curriculum and professional development vendors to test out models and share feedback and lessons learned with others.

Potential Challenges Related to K–12 System and Teacher Preparation Actions

Moving forward, LDOE faces several potential challenges related to its ongoing K–12 academic and teacher preparation reforms. First, LDOE must ensure that stakeholders not only are aware of how Louisiana is defining high-quality curricula and assessments, but also have professional development opportunities that will allow stakeholders to implement these curricula and assessments thoughtfully and in ways that align with their intended use. Second, the fact that the timeline for adoption of new standards and assessments in science and social studies may not align with curriculum adoption, or state reviews identifying high-quality curricula aligned with those standards, could create anxiety among educators. Lastly, while LDOE has done much work to build understanding and support for new requirements for teacher preparation institutions, the considerable shifts in these requirements—for example, requirements for programs to integrate yearlong residencies—may be challenging for some preparation providers to implement quickly. At the same time, LDOE has given the majority of teacher preparation providers an opportunity to test out aspects of the new requirements that have recently been passed into policy.

Graduation Pathways: Policies, Actions, and Challenges

Louisiana students face a number of challenges to success in their transition from high school to college and the workplace. For example, in 2016, Louisiana ranked 47th in the nation in terms of the percentage of residents with two- and four-year college degrees, and less than a quarter of Louisiana adults over 25 completed bachelor's degree requirements. This puts the state and its workers in a precarious situation, given estimates that 65 percent of jobs nationally will require postsecondary education and training by 2020 (Carnevale, Smith, and Strohl, 2013). In addition, while many of the projected new jobs in Louisiana were "middle-skill" (requiring high school and some additional training) (National Skills Coalition, 2015), not enough Louisiana students were obtaining the certifications necessary to get these jobs and meet the growing needs of employers in the state.

Key Graduation Pathway Strategies

Louisiana has leaned heavily on mandates to ensure that all students pursue a pathway to college or career. In particular, the state requires high schools to ensure that all students pursue a pathway to either an industry-based certificate or postsecondary enrollment (or both). Publicly reported data for high schools include a broad array of indicators related to college and workplace readiness. Importantly, these indicators place equal value on students' pursuit of college versus their pursuit of a career, which officials regard as a starting point for supporting students and families to place equal value on either option. LDOE has also fostered partnerships with colleges and industry to support the development and scaling of both career and college pathways, and LDOE has made considerable efforts to communicate processes by which partners and stakeholders can implement LDOE policies.

Table S.3
Graduation Pathway Actions in Louisiana

Action	Policy Lever	Early Progress
1. Require all high school students to pursue a pathway toward an industry-based certificate, postsecondary enrollment, or both.	Mandate	• Starting in 2014, Louisiana required students to pursue one (or both) of two possible high school diplomas: (1) the Taylor Opportunity Program for Students (TOPS) University Pathway that aligns course requirements to a state four-year higher education scholarship and (2) the Jump Start TOPS Tech Pathway that culminates in an industry-endorsed credential.
2. Implement graduation requirements that facilitate links with college and technical school admission and financial aid.	Mandate	• In 2013, Louisiana mandated that all students take the ACT as a requirement of graduation. • In 2015, Louisiana made completion of the Free Application for Federal Student Aid (FAFSA) a graduation requirement starting in 2018.
3. Provide public data to hold Louisiana schools accountable on performance related to college and career readiness, valuing both tracks equally.	Mandate	• Indicators on school report cards related to graduation pathways include ACT scores, graduation rates, AP scores, college enrollment, and completion of professional certifications. • Schools receive equal credit in indicators for both college and career outcomes, with the same recognition for students for who obtain a 3 or more on the AP exam and students who earn an advanced industry credential.
4. Create course pathways that lead to high-quality industry credentials and preparation for certain college majors.	Resource alignment	• LDOE developed 49 Jump Start career and technical education pathways related to construction, industry, health care, technology, and more. • LDOE developed several college preparation pathways including pre-engineering and micro-enterprise.
5. Enable Louisiana teachers to have the credentials needed to implement the Jump Start pathways.	Resource alignment	• LDOE required that all Jump Start teachers have the industry credential for the courses that they teach. • 850 teachers received 1,000 industry credentials at LDOE-sponsored summer institutes, and the state streamlined the teacher licensing process to allow industry professionals to directly enter the teacher workforce via a Career and Technical Trade and Industrial Education (CTTIE) certificate.

Table S.3—continued

Action	Policy Lever	Early Progress
6. Curate and fund access to quality external courses and credential opportunities.	Incentive	• Students now have access to courses provided by local colleges, industry, and online learning as part of their high school degree. • These external courses are often used for career and technical education, ACT preparation, and other enrichment courses. • Jump Start pathways prepare students to obtain industry certifications during their high school degree.
7. Draw on industry and higher education partners to select and create high school course pathways, based on regional workforce needs.	Communication and planning processes	• Regional committees involving schools, community colleges, workforce boards, and industry leaders select and design the priority pathways offered in Louisiana's high schools. • Involvement of regional industry is meant to create coherence among K–12 job preparation, student opportunities, and industry needs.

Policy-Related Graduation Pathway Actions

To address education and workforce fulfillment challenges, as well as inequities in education and employment opportunities based on racial and socioeconomic diversity, LDOE has developed seven specific actions to fulfill three goals: (1) improve career readiness to prepare students for "success in a Louisiana workplace"; (2) improve college readiness to promote "success in postsecondary education"; and (3) create more options for postsecondary education finance to boost "economic opportunity." These actions, policy levers, and early progress are documented in Table S.3.

Challenges Related to Graduation Pathways

While Louisiana has made significant progress in developing its career pathways strategies and initial rollout of key actions, challenges to implementation remain. For instance, students of low socioeconomic status and African American students face impediments to achieving full equity of opportunity for college attendance; indeed, most state-funded scholarship recipients in recent years, for example, have been white and middle to upper-middle class. State budgeting inconsistencies strain the chance of future success as well. For example, Louisiana has struggled to fully fund its college scholarship program in recent years, despite its widespread popularity. Finally, the state faces regional variations in implementation among public schools—differences in resources, leadership, and capacity among school districts have made implementation of these new initiatives uneven.

Cross-Cutting Themes Related to State Reforms

Seven cross-cutting themes emerged from Louisiana's changes to ECE programs, K–12 academic instruction, teacher preparation, and pathways to graduation.

Clarity of vision around what constitutes "high-quality" teaching and learning. LDOE leaders recognize the value of the information that is conveyed through their selection of measures and indicators that are used for public reporting. In particular, the state assesses the quality of and publishes ratings of ECE programs, instructional materials, professional development providers, schools, and teacher preparation programs. In both ECE and K–12 education, curriculum reviews based on quality rubrics and a list of recommended curricula are intended to provide a model for what content and tasks are aligned with standards. While both ECE and K–12 education systems include teacher evaluation processes mandated by the state, the Classroom Assessment Scoring System (CLASS) observation rubric plays a particularly important role in how quality instruction is defined for early childhood educators. In graduation pathways, school performance measures give equal weight to success in college preparation and completion of high-quality industry credentials, signaling that the state values both of these pathways equally.

Close adherence to intended theory of implementation apart from federal mandates. LDOE has articulated an intended theory of implementation that begins with testing and information gathering in regard to a particular initiative, followed by extensive use of data to identify points of coherence and alignment and to work to scale up the initiative across the state through partnerships. Ideally, full implementation of a mandate is put in place only after those prior steps have been taken to ensure both that LDOE has an idea about how full implementation might look—based on its data gathering efforts—and that partners have engaged in processes that will then be passed into law and policy. Then, the state develops and communicates planning processes for stakeholders to implement policies. We see more piloting and testing for policy areas that fall under LDOE's control (i.e., areas relatively free from federal mandates), including ECE and teacher preparation. Other aspects of LDOE's theory of implementation are reflected across multiple areas, and we discuss these areas in more detail in our themes below, including LDOE's external partnerships with both educators and other stakeholders, as well as efforts to ensure coherence and alignment.

Close involvement with educators to gather feedback and promote buy-in. State leaders have developed a variety of communication approaches, both formal and informal, and many of them focus on seeking feedback from teachers and other educators. By conveying the message that the state values these educators' input, state officials were able to gather information while also promoting educator engagement and support. In particular, K–12 and teacher preparation have defined roles for educators selected and trained by the state, who then provide information and professional development to their teacher colleagues, as well as participate in state initiatives. Such roles include teacher leader advisers, teacher leaders, content leaders, and mentor teachers.

Partnerships with external stakeholders to provide information and support scale. In every area of its reform, LDOE works closely with external partners to expand their capacity and reach. These partnerships serve two roles. First, they help LDOE gather information and foster relationships that support buy-in. Second, they have enabled LDOE to engage with private providers in a way that allows the state to maintain oversight and influence. For example, the state has engaged with private ECE providers and has developed mechanisms to regulate their work. The state's rating system for private textbook companies for curriculum and for private teacher development training organizations has enabled the state to incentivize private-sector program developers and vendors to create products and programs that are aligned with the state's goals. Workforce boards and industry leaders have helped to select career pathways, and LDOE relies on external industry certification for credentialing students.

Coherence and alignment among mandates, incentives, and resources. LDOE leaders identified several ways in which their work has been designed to create a coordinated set of policies and practices that focus on student learning from the earliest ages through graduation and entry into postsecondary institutions. First, LDOE notes that the organization of its own department encourages coordination and integration of messages. Second, LDOE has sought to align mandates with incentives, resources, and tools in all areas of its system. Lastly, the guidebooks that LDOE provides to all stakeholders are intended to be a single, clear source of information about state mandates and associated incentives and resources, and state officials from multiple divisions from within LDOE weigh in on these guidebooks.

Promotion of equity through incentives and resources. Louisiana, like other states, has noted a lack of equitable access to high-quality opportunities. In some geographical regions, parent ECE choice is extremely limited. This means that the publication of information about provider quality may not always enable parents to select high-quality options for their children. The state is working to reduce ECE inequities by increasing financial assistance to families through the Child Care Assistance Program (CCAP), but challenges to addressing the lack of high-quality choices in some geographic areas persist. Efforts to ensure that high-quality resources are "open" and available to all schools and educators are intended to address equity concerns. Equity challenges also remain in the uneven college and workplace opportunities for students of diverse ethnicities and low socioeconomic status.

Quality ratings for both processes and outcomes, with an increasing emphasis on outcomes as students get older. Louisiana emphasizes quality ratings as a form of accountability, issuing mandates for public reporting of results and creating incentives for educators and institutions to focus on key aspects of curriculum and student outcomes. Yet, our examination of quality indicates that the relative importance of student outcomes—in comparison with processes that might be connected to those outcomes—increases with student age. This is consistent with a broader goal of ensuring that students have access to high-quality instructional experiences early on while developing the knowledge and skills needed for postsecondary success.

Key Potential Implementation Issues

Our work suggests three key implementation challenges that could detract from state efforts.

Equity issues are intertwined with the capacity of collaborative networks, early childhood centers, and schools to undertake state reforms. LDOE's ambitious reforms require considerable changes to the education system in Louisiana. All of these changes require high-capacity partners and school capacity to build educator knowledge. LDOE has begun taking some of the steps necessary to build capacity by putting in place such structures as early childhood networks and placing emphasis on the development of educator expertise. The extent to which the state can identify which centers and schools are falling behind will be key to the provision of additional support.

Educator preparation places a strong emphasis on practical experience, but the effectiveness of this approach has not yet been determined. The importance of practical, on-the-ground experience for candidates who are training to become educators has been underscored by changes such as the Early Childhood Ancillary Certificate, which includes a requirement for practical experience, and K–12 teacher preparation, which includes a residency requirement for aspiring teachers. This emphasis reflects state leaders' beliefs that offering prospective teachers and instructors the opportunity to practice their craft in real classrooms is likely to promote instructional quality. Measuring the success of these reforms will require the regular collection of data on performance of program graduates and other measures of teacher preparation quality. As part of teacher preparation reforms, a quality rating system for preparation providers of K–12 teachers was passed into policy in 2017, and results from that system will provide evidence on whether these state reforms are paying off. However, the state does not yet have a similar mechanism in place for evaluating the quality of programs that will provide the Early Childhood Ancillary Certificate.

The state's tradition of local control likely has both benefits and drawbacks. Although Louisiana had adopted mandates to effect change, it has balanced these mandates with the state's long tradition of ensuring that local education agencies have significant autonomy and influence over policies and practices related to education. This approach may have helped to promote widespread support for the state's efforts, and it may also facilitate local experimentation with different approaches, which in turn could provide lessons to other educators or schools. The state's various networks provide one means to promote collaboration and communication around these local lessons. At the same time, however, decentralization can lead to uneven implementation and has the potential to exacerbate inequities.

Final Thoughts and Next Steps

Because our work is based only on available documentation and interviews with state officials, our analysis is limited. For example, any potential implementation challenges that we discuss likely do not capture all the challenges that stakeholders—teachers, school leaders, and parents—face in interpreting, translating, and acting on state policies. Moreover, we cannot draw any clear conclusions about how educational improvements or increases in student achievement could be tied to state policies, nor which particular state policies or actions might be driving any improvements. In our follow-on research, we will explore these connections with implementation and student outcomes.

Acknowledgments

We would like to thank the Louisiana Department of Education staff who generously took time out of their busy schedules to talk with us about their work, as well as review our report for accuracy. We would also like to thank Elizabeth Thornton for her assistance with data collection and Naomi Hale and Nirabh Koirala for their transcription help. This report would not be possible without the support of our sponsor, the Baton Rouge Area Foundation, via a generous donation from Bloomberg Philanthropies. In addition, a special thanks to Joanne Weiss and Stephani Wrabel, who reviewed this report and provided great ideas and feedback that guided our report revisions.

Abbreviations

AP   Advanced Placement

BESE   Louisiana Board of Elementary and Secondary Education

CCAP   Child Care Assistance Program

CDA   Child Development Associate

CLASS   Classroom Assessment Scoring System

CTE   career and technical education

DCFS   Department of Children and Family Services

ECE   early childhood education

ECEN   Early Childhood Care and Education Network

ELA   English language arts

ESSA   Every Student Succeeds Act

FAFSA   Free Application for Federal Student Aid

K–12   kindergarten through 12th grade

LDOE   Louisiana Department of Education

LSU   Louisiana State University

NAEP   National Assessment of Educational Progress

NCLB   No Child Left Behind Act of 2001

PARCC   Partnership for Assessment of Readiness for College and Career

pre-K   pre-kindergarten

RTTT   Race to the Top

STEM   science, technology, engineering, and mathematics

TOPS   Taylor Opportunity Program for Students

CHAPTER ONE

Introduction

Since the turn of the century, the United States has experienced a sea change of accountability legislation aimed at making schools and teachers more accountable for student learning. The No Child Left Behind Act of 2001 (NCLB) required more state-mandated testing in reading and mathematics and public reporting of test results to gauge achievement gaps between subgroups, and it also required states to set specific sanctions for lower-performing schools. Beginning in 2010, the Race to the Top (RTTT) initiative provided federal monetary incentives for a select group of states that passed additional accountability legislation in the form of more rigorous state standards modeled from the Common Core State Standards, standards-aligned tests, and evaluation systems that took into account student achievement in judging teacher and school performance.

Despite this proliferation of accountability legislation across the United States, states have taken a variety of paths in terms of the specific legislation and accompanying policies, likely driven somewhat by variations in state capacity and available federal and state funding. For example, many states use different tests and have different definitions of what counts as proficient on those tests, as well as what measures to use and how to calculate student growth for teacher and school evaluation systems.[1] Yet, while some research has taken stock of differing state laws and policies passed in response to federal accountability laws, little research has taken a holistic look at how specific state sys-

---

[1] For some sense of the differences among these state policies, see Cronin et al. (2007) or National Council on Teacher Quality (2017).

tems have made sense of all the federal legislation to set their own path toward supporting improvements in student outcomes. Furthermore, while a number of studies have noted the gap between ambitious, high-demand federal education policies and the necessary capacity to implement them,[2] we have not identified any research that documents in detail how states communicate with stakeholders, implement planning processes, and attempt to build capacity to meet the much higher bar set by new state standards and their accompanying testing and evaluation systems.

This report is an attempt to track education reform efforts in the wake of NCLB and RTTT in a single state: Louisiana. Few other states have experienced as much political and social turbulence in their education systems over the past several years. Even before Hurricane Katrina wrought costly devastation in Louisiana in 2005, Louisiana was (and remains) one of the poorest states in the nation (Bishaw and Benson, 2017). Following Hurricane Katrina, the state engaged in highly publicized work to take over New Orleans's schools and turn them over to charter management organizations. Yet, New Orleans is only a very small piece of the state's larger reform landscape. In spite of backlash and opposition to the state's adoption of Common Core State Standards and standards-aligned assessments, Louisiana has succeeded in making some broad changes across its education system, with the overarching goal of improving outcomes for students across the education system, from birth to grade 12. Some reforms have been extensive in scope, including restructuring the system of authority of early childhood providers and adding external industry certifications to high school diplomas. Other reforms have been structurally modest, but are connected with changes in teachers' work in schools, including curriculum reforms that may be responsible for increased uptake of the Eureka Math curriculum across the state (Kaufman, Thompson, and Opfer, 2016). In addition, Louisiana has recently observed steady improvements in student outcomes, including improvements in ACT scores and Advanced Placement (AP) course completions (The College Board, 2014; Nobles, 2017).

---

[2]   See, for example, Ladd (2017) and McGuinn (2012).

Focus on State Actions and Policy Levers

In this report, we provide an overview of Louisiana's reforms in four major areas: early childhood education (ECE), kindergarten through 12th grade (K–12) academics, K–12 teacher preparation, and graduation pathways to college and career. We describe the key goals, actions, and strategies in each of these areas. We also consider how state actions reflect four "levers" that the Louisiana Department of Education (LDOE) has used to pursue state goals in each major area:

- **Mandates:** Rules or requirements for individuals or organizations.
- **Resources:** Tools or information aligned with goals and intended to support individuals or organizations in meeting those goals.
- **Incentives:** Inducements intended to encourage individuals or organizations to follow mandates and utilize resources.
- **Communication and planning processes:** Communication networks, messages, technical assistance, and collaborative structures to both inform and gather inputs from stakeholders.

We particularly examine how that fourth lever—communication and planning processes—may act as a policy lever for change. Policy researchers have explored various "levers" that might be used productively by state policymakers—depending on their context—to support education improvements, including mandates or regulation, financial incentives, and shifts to structures of authority (Fuhrman, Clune, and Elmore, 1991; McDonnell and Elmore, 1987). More recently, Coburn, Hill, and Spillane (2016) focused on the importance of two primary state strategies to support improvements to teaching and learning: (1) alignment of learning standards with other aspects of teaching and learning, including assessments, professional development, curriculum materials, and teacher evaluation; and (2) metrics and measures intended to increase school and teacher accountability for student learning. Yet, as noted by Honig (2006), policymaking is a complex process that depends deeply on interactions among policies, people, and places. These interactions imply the need to utilize thoughtful and comprehensive communication strategies as one additional strategy or tool to support policy implementation.

LDOE's communications with key stakeholders appear to be infused in LDOE work from beginning to end as a policy lever and tool that has not been explicitly observed in other policy literature. One aspect of LDOE's communication efforts that is especially consistent across areas of its work is their streamlined, coherent nature. One state official with whom we spoke noted that when she began her work at LDOE in 2012, at the same time as the new state superintendent, school districts received multiple unrelated communications and messages about LDOE work and priorities. She commented that there were many different programs within LDOE at the time, but there was not "an aligned set of priorities across departments." She said, "We needed to get control of communications within the building and outside the building. There were 600 people on staff and about 300 were emailing districts about something." At the time, LDOE leadership made the decision that every message from the department would go through the state superintendent's chief of staff. One staff member with whom we spoke conceded that while such centralization might seem "archaic," it "reset a norm of who we are and what we do as an agency." She continued:

> What we are not is a bunch of individual actors taking individual actions on behalf of individual programs. We are about improving the results for kids in the state. And everything is under that umbrella. We're trying to do that in a coordinated and connected way. And so that very aggressive stance for the first year really helped reorient our team in a quick way to say, "We have to be organized. We have to be connected. We have to create structures internally."

This effort to streamline communications was a catalyst for the changing structures and routines that LDOE has set up with various stakeholders in the LDOE system. As one staff member noted, requiring that all communication come from one source "forced us very, very fast to create a district planning newsletter, create a monthly district planning call, and create the collaboration structures. It forced us to have to find structures to communicate collectively." Specifically, LDOE has created structures for communicating similar messages about key state strategies and reform efforts with district superintendents, academic supervisors, district data managers, technology coordinators, principals, teacher leaders, counselors, early childhood community network leads, teacher preparation leaders, and local workforce boards. Modes of communication include weekly or monthly newsletters to districts, school counselors, teacher leaders, and early childhood providers and networks; monthly district planning calls and webinars; and events that include statewide and regional collaboratives, trainings, and a Teacher Leader Summit each year. In addition, districts and ECE network agencies participate in regular calls with state staff who support their regional networks. While every email no longer filters through a single person at LDOE, state officials from multiple offices weigh in on various communications to ensure that offices are communicating in a clear and aligned way. One staff member noted that ensuring integrated and aligned communication is still a challenge: "Everybody's working really hard, so it is a daily struggle for us to make sure we're looping in the right people."

LDOE's communications are also reflected in a particular theory of policy implementation that some state officials described to us. Specifically, LDOE officials noted that they aim first to pilot and test their ideas with external partners. This testing is not only an information-gathering mechanism, but also helps LDOE identify models for its work and establish some initial buy-in. Officials also spoke about work to intentionally align aspects of reforms together, connecting the content of reforms with aligned resources and tools. With external partnerships, they also seek to find models and supports that will emphasize the content of a given reform. Ideally, mandates are fully implemented only after this capacity-building, piloting, alignment, and partnership work has been completed, although mandates have sometimes necessarily preceded those phases. Lastly, LDOE creates planning process documents for numerous stakeholder groups and puts those documents online to support policy implementation. While all LDOE's work does not follow this theory of implementation perfectly, we did identify aspects of this theory in all areas of its work.

Figure 1.1 summarizes this theory of implementation. Importantly, multiple aspects of this process rely on the fourth policy lever described above: communication and planning processes. While this lever is the last one we listed, such communication and planning processes are inserted alongside various levers and at different timepoints in policymaking processes. Specifically, LDOE communicates with partners at various points on the pathway toward policy implementation, from connecting with organizations and individuals to test out ideas, to scaling reforms in cooperation with external partners, to communicating and planning processes intended to support leaders, educators, and other school staff at various levels in the education system.

Figure 1.1
Louisiana Department of Education's Theory of Implementation

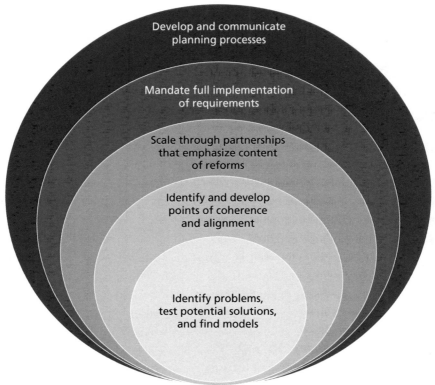

Whether this theory of implementation is working exactly as intended has yet to be determined. In subsequent reports that are part of our overall study, we will consider how Louisiana policies are being translated by key stakeholders, as well as how state actions are leading to changes in stakeholder behaviors and student outcomes.

Purposes of This Report

This report has three main purposes: (1) to track Louisiana's reform efforts and early signals of the potential success of those efforts; (2) to set the stage for more in-depth analyses of state policy implementation and student outcomes that might be linked to Louisiana's reform efforts; and (3) to take stock of the differences among the strategies and levers that Louisiana has relied on to reform various areas of its education system, which may have further implications for research on how policies might link with innovation and educational improvement. We describe each of those purposes in greater depth below.

Purpose 1: To track reform efforts in a state department of education that has been receiving some recent attention for new policies and some promising early results. For example, Louisiana is one of only a few states that has developed or recommended curricula aligned with its standards that are open and accessible to all, as well as developed a large suite of tools and professional development trainings designed to help teachers use recommended curricula and assess progress on that curricula (Chiefs for Change, 2017; Westendorf, 2017; Will, 2017). A recent RAND report suggested that Louisiana teachers are teaching and thinking about their work in ways that are more aligned with their state standards compared with teachers in other states (Kaufman, Thompson, and Opfer, 2016). Louisiana has also received some recent attention for the high quality of its accountability plan to address the federal Every Student Succeeds Act (ESSA), which was approved by the U.S. Department of Education in August and passed into policy through the Louisiana Board of Elementary and Secondary Education (BESE) in October 2017 (Phenicie, 2017; REL Southwest, 2017). The textbox provides more information on the state's

Louisiana's ESSA Plan

The Every Student Succeeds Act (ESSA) is the newest iteration of Elementary and Secondary Education legislation and the successor to the No Child Left Behind Act of 2001. Compared with NCLB, ESSA gives states somewhat more flexibility on certain aspects of accountability, but it still requires states to retain challenging standards, assess students at particular grade levels, and provide public reports on schoolwide student performance on assessments. Louisiana's plan can be characterized by high expectations— it explicitly sets a high bar for all students, particularly those in historically underserved subgroups.

The state's ESSA plan reflects "three critical shifts" (LDOE, 2017d). First, Louisiana is trying to raise the bar for quality; it will be more challenging for schools to earn an "A" in Louisiana's letter grade system. An "A" rating will be connected to higher achievement levels, graduation rates, and ACT scores than what was required previously. Second, the plan places a greater value on individual student progress, including adding a new growth index to school ratings that assesses the extent to which students are on the path to mastery and advancing relative to their peers. In this new growth index, students who do not achieve mastery receive a growth target for the following year, which provides both educators and parents with transparent information about their rate of progress. Students who do not meet their growth targets will be compared with similar peers using Louisiana's value added system. These students will then receive a comparison score based on how they are doing relative to this peer group, rather than the initial growth target. Lastly, Louisiana's ESSA plan emphasizes enrichment; 5 percent of a school's performance score will take into account the "interests and opportunities" that schools provide to students, including diverse learning opportunities, such as foreign languages, performing and visual arts, technology, AP courses, and extracurricular activities and clubs. All three requirements are intended to be gradually implemented over the next several years.

ESSA plan. In addition, the National Institute for Early Education Research has reported on the major changes to Louisiana's early childhood system, which are intended to shift LDOE from an organization focused on K–12 education to a "Birth–12th grade organization" (National Institute for Early Education Research, 2015). Yet, despite the attention that Louisiana has received, it still faces significant challenges that we point out throughout this report. Furthermore, Louisiana is grappling with many of the same challenges that are confronting states across the United States, and its experience can offer an example of how one state is attempting to address those challenges.

Purpose 2: To set the stage for more in-depth analyses of state policy implementation and student outcomes in Louisiana that might be linked to the state's reform efforts. We do not yet have the data we would need to link Louisiana's reform efforts to any changes in student outcomes. This report is therefore not intended to suggest a prescriptive approach to state policy in any of the areas we have investigated. Instead, by describing Louisiana's approaches in each area, we hope both to provide an example of how one state is addressing challenges to students' success and also set the stage for future analyses we are planning now. Those analyses will examine how Louisiana reforms (1) are being implemented—or interpreted, translated, and/or acted upon—by school districts and other stakeholder organizations; (2) are connected with changes in what stakeholders do to support students; and (3) are connected with a range of student outcomes. We plan to release a series of reports on our implementation and outcomes analyses in 2019.

Purpose 3: To take stock of the differences among the strategies and levers that Louisiana has relied on to reform various areas of its education system, which may have further implications for research on how policies might link with innovation and educational improvement. With the passage of ESSA, there is increasing pressure on state departments of education (DOEs) to find ways to support innovation and improvement. The role of state DOEs in U.S. educational systems has never been straightforward; the immense variability in governance structures, political systems, and state capacities has made understanding state policy and its relationship to student

Data and Methods

This report is based on several data sources. First, we draw heavily on documentation of state policy efforts, including documents provided to us by LDOE, publicly available documents from the LDOE website (http://www.louisianabelieves.com/), and media reports. We also consulted legislative records and reports produced by other organizations, where appropriate. Second, we drew on data from interviews with 22 state officials that were conducted in September and October 2017. This report also draws on research already completed as part of a previous RAND report by Kaufman, Thompson, and Opfer (2016) that examined how Louisiana state strategies might be linked to teachers' knowledge of their standards and classroom practices. Lastly, informal observations of a state-led regional teacher and leader professional development convening that we attended in September 2017 provided important context that both informed our interview questions and supported our analyses.

For our document review, our aim was to identify the key strategies the state appeared to be using to support education in four areas: ECE, K–12 academics, K–12 teacher preparation, and graduation pathways. For each of these areas, we created summaries based on available documentation, drawing mostly upon documents available on the LDOE website, media reports, and in BESE policy documents. For each area, we created a summary that then informed the protocols we developed for our interviews with LDOE staff. For example, for ECE, our document review pointed to local networks and the public program rating system—as well as legislation—as integral parts of LDOE's ECE strategy. Thus, in our interviews with LDOE's ECE staff, we particularly probed to understand the role of local networks and how the rating system worked.

We conducted interviews individually and in person with LDOE staff, and the interviews were recorded so that we could check notes from the interviews for accuracy. Beyond asking about themes that had also been identified in the document review, we asked state officials about their priorities, key levers or strategies that

Data and Methods—continued

have helped them make progress on their priorities, and challenges they anticipate going forward, among other topics. Transcripts of interviews were created based on the recordings and interview notes. We examined these transcripts and coded them according to policy levers—i.e., mandates, resources, incentives, and communications— and key state actions. For example, for interviews with officials that focus on K–12 academics, we coded for any discussion of curricula, given that we had identified that as a key state action. However, at the same time, we revised key actions over time based on additional coding and analysis.

Because our work is based only on available documentation and interviews with state officials, our analysis is limited. It does not address perceptions among those in the Louisiana legislature or BESE. Nor does it include perspectives of those that are the targets of Louisiana reforms, including educators, agencies, parents, and students. Therefore, any potential implementation challenges that we discuss may not capture all the challenges that stakeholders face in interpreting, translating, and acting on state policies. In addition, we cannot draw any clear conclusions about how educational improvements or increases in student achievement could be tied to state policies, nor which state policies or actions—in particular— might be driving any improvements. In our follow-on research, we will explore these connections with implementation and student outcomes.

outcomes a challenging task. Seashore Louis and colleagues (2008), for instance, noted that state DOEs have "struggled" to find the right long-term policy mechanisms to meaningfully shift teaching and learning in the classroom, which is notoriously resistant to change efforts that come from beyond the school. In their classic study of state policy implementation, McDonnell and McLaughlin (1982) described some of the forces that constrain state educational agencies (SEAs), noting their organizational fragmentation and their reliance on state political structures and annual budgets. These system characteristics often lead to narrow, short-term vision and a limited sense of coordination and coherence in SEAs.

Roadmap for the Report

We begin in Chapter Two with a discussion of the key Louisiana actions and levers related to reforms in early childhood education. Chapter Three examines similar levers and efforts related to the K–12 system and K–12 teacher preparation, followed by a focus in Chapter Four on graduation pathways. In each chapter, the levers we specifically consider are mandates, resources, incentives, and communication. Additionally, at the end of each chapter, we outline a set of potential implementation challenges that we think are implied by Louisiana's actions. These are potential challenges identified through our discussions with state officials, as well as through our own reflection. They are not meant to be exhaustive, and some challenges we outline may not be ones that stakeholders in school districts or other organizations would identify. We plan to use those challenges to help us consider what implementation measures to focus on in our subsequent implementation data collection and analyses. We conclude in Chapter Five with a summary of findings across the four major areas and discussion of next steps.

CHAPTER TWO

Early Childhood Education

Many students in Louisiana enter kindergarten lacking important skills to help prepare them for school success. For example, roughly half of kindergartners statewide performed below grade level on kindergarten fall literacy assessments, as measured from 2012 to 2016 (LDOE, 2013a, 2016b). More than half of third graders failed to achieve mastery in reading or mathematics on a statewide assessment (LDOE, 2016c). This shortfall in school readiness skills is related, in part, to the variation in ECE programs that children may experience, including unequal access to high-quality programs and educators. Louisiana has about 1,500 publicly funded ECE programs, which may greatly differ in quality. Furthermore, families may not have full information from a single source on program aspects such as safety, quality, and use of curriculum, or a listing of all available programs to determine the best choices for their children.

Since 2012, Louisiana has engaged in a series of ECE reforms to address these challenges, based on a theory of implementation described in Chapter One that includes engagement with partners to test out and pilot processes; work to closely align mandates, resources, and incentives; and communication with all stakeholders about planning processes that can support policy implementation. Specifically, LDOE, in partnership with the Governor's Office and BESE, has set forth to build a common understanding of what ECE program quality looks like in order to achieve better student outcomes and to refine this understanding through piloting efforts and community input. LDOE is supporting this movement toward consistent, high-quality programs with a set of mandates combined with aligned resources and incentives to facilitate program quality improvement, measurement, and access. Integral to this approach is the communication with and involvement of key partners, such as ECE community networks throughout the state, during the planning and implementation phases.

These reforms have redefined and unified the ECE system and have also created a shared vision of high-quality early learning focused on improving kindergarten readiness for Louisiana's students from birth to age five. This chapter discusses LDOE's vision and goals for the ECE system and ways in which reforms have mandated, provided resources for, incentivized, and communicated these goals and initiatives to a diverse early childhood community. In particular, our findings highlight how the state has used key mandates and funding incentives, along with collaborative efforts with community partners, to further its goals for reforming Louisiana's ECE system.

Key Goals and Actions

A defining goal for the LDOE Early Childhood Office is to ensure that children start school ready to learn, as noted in conversations with multiple state officials and in LDOE communications (LDOE, 2017a). A key component of that goal is creating a shared vision of high-quality ECE teaching and classroom practice (LDOE, 2017b) and a definition of kindergarten readiness that encompasses cognitive, social, emotional, and motor skills (LDOE, undated-a). At the same time, Louisiana seeks to facilitate parent choice of and access to high-quality care, regardless of public funding source. One state official stated, "If you have that kind of platform, where you have a basic sense of quality and access, and families have a basic sense of access—and can do so having reviewed transparent, objective information about the center—then you have a system of incentives that compels performance."

The foundational legislation related to recent ECE system reforms is the 2012 Early Childhood Care and Education Act (also known as "Act 3"). This legislation sought to unify a complex and fragmented system of early childhood programs in the state by shifting governance and accountability for publicly funded programs serving children birth to age five under a single umbrella through the Louisiana BESE, with a common goal of preparing children for kindergarten. The publicly funded programs exist in three types of centers: (1) school-based pre-kindergarten (pre-K), (2) Head Start, and (3) child care serving low-income children who are funded through the Child Care Assistance Program (CCAP). The law also mandated that LDOE and BESE create an assessment and accountability system for some ECE centers (known as "Type III" centers[1]) to improve quality and create a system of local ECE networks that provide coordinated enrollment across programs to provide access to high-quality programs for families. Act 3 specifies:

> In order to significantly improve outcomes at all levels of the state's educational system, it is imperative that standards for, and expectations of, our early childhood programs be raised to levels that will promote kindergarten readiness and sustain lifelong learning and achievement. (Louisiana State Legislature, 2012)

While Act 3 set a broad vision, the details for implementing the vision and defining quality were left to LDOE and BESE. Before these governance and accountability reform efforts began, ECE programs fell under different governing authority and thus could have different standards, funding, and accountability affecting center-based care. Pre-K centers fell under LDOE, and child care centers were administered by the Department of Children and Family Services (DCFS). Head Start centers also fell within DCFS purview for some oversight, although they are federally funded.

To further unify the system, a key follow-up step to Act 3 was to pass legislation in 2014 to move all ECE program licensing (and program enrollment, as we discuss later) under LDOE, shifting Head Start and state child care program licensing functions over from

---

[1]   Under Louisiana law, Type III ECE centers are those that directly or indirectly receive public funds from any source other than nutrition programs. Only Type III centers are required to participate in the new rating system. Type I centers, defined as those operated by religious organizations and receiving no public funds, and Type II centers, defined as those receiving public funds only through the food and nutrition program, are not part of the rating system.

DCFS. As one official noted, "This doesn't work if we don't get licensing [under LDOE]," because licensing is what drives much of a center's behavior, and the state wanted all centers to have similar accountability. Officials explained that a unique feature of this legislation was that it included Head Start programs, which must now meet the same academic performance requirements as state pre-K and child care programs, although Head Start funding authority remains at the federal level. This major reform resulted in BESE gaining policy authority over all state ECE programs, and funding authority for all except Head Start.[2] Furthermore, since 2012, the state has engaged in a set of key actions to create and communicate a shared understanding of quality; support and incentivize improved classroom quality; and foster parent choice of high-quality care.

The key actions LDOE has taken to create a unified system through legislation and other strategies are summarized in Table 2.1. In addition, since 2012, the staff of the LDOE Early Childhood Office has increased almost tenfold to administer and oversee these increased departmental responsibilities (LDOE, 2017c).

We discuss these actions and related initiatives in more detail below in the context of mandates, quality incentives, and planning processes. Figure 2.1 summarizes the timeline for the major policies and activities that were part of this work.

Mandates

In the course of implementing laws and policy directives, LDOE has created both mandated initiatives and resources and incentives to encourage adoption of practices to improve quality. We first describe two mandates that are part of the ECE accountability system: a uniform rating system for all centers and creation of a new certificate program as a minimum level of preparation for lead teachers. While these

---

[2]   One state ECE program that was not moved under BESE authority is Early Steps, a program for infants and toddlers with developmental delays or disabilities that is administered by the Department of Health.

Table 2.1
Early Childhood Education Actions in Louisiana

Action	Policy Lever
1. Create and require a unified rating system, connected to licensure and funding for all publicly funded centers, to provide information on center quality.	Mandate
2. Strengthen lead teacher preparation requirements through a new ECE teacher credential: the Early Childhood Ancillary Certificate.	Mandate
3. Signal to ECE staff which curricula, formative assessments, and professional development are high-quality and standards-aligned.	Resource alignment
4. Increase funding for Child Care Assistance Program (CCAP) subsidies to increase parity and encourage diversity in types of centers serving publicly funded children.	Incentive
5. Provide funding incentives tied to higher quality ratings, teacher training, and curriculum use.	Incentive
6. Define and require community networks for administration and communication, including coordinated ECE program enrollment for families.	Communication and planning processes

mandates set a high bar for early childhood programs, the mandates were preceded by a year of practice and piloting to prepare stakeholders and learn more about how to best support the mandates when they went into full effect.

Action 1. Create and require a unified rating system, connected to licensure and funding for all publicly funded centers, that provides information on center quality.

According to a state official we spoke with, "The core piece of our work is this universal, non-optional rating system." LDOE presentations to community stakeholders note that the department is creating a "unified rating system indicative of child outcomes" (LDOE, 2017c) and that this system is purposefully connected to center licensure as a form of accountability. As part of licensing, Type III centers (i.e., those that receive public funding) must now meet *academic approval*, or a set of performance standards, and participate in the community

Figure 2.1
Timeline for Major Policies and Activities in Early Childhood Education

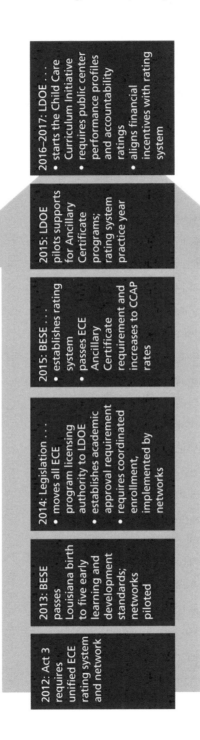

2012: Act 3 requires unified ECE rating system and network

2013: BESE passes Louisiana birth to five early learning and development standards; networks piloted

2014: Legislation . . .
• moves all ECE program licensing authority to LDOE
• establishes academic approval requirement
• requires coordinated enrollment, implemented by networks

2015: BESE . . .
• establishes rating system
• passes ECE Ancillary Certificate requirement and increases to CCAP rates

2015: LDOE pilots supports for Ancillary Certificate programs; rating system practice year

2016–2017: LDOE . . .
• starts the Child Care Curriculum Initiative
• requires public center performance profiles and accountability ratings
• aligns financial incentives with rating system

RAND *RR2303-2.1*

network system (described below). The ratings are a means to hold all programs accountable to the same requirements as a condition of licensing, regardless of public funding source. Furthermore, academic approval is also a condition for funding for state pre-kindergarten (pre-K). As one state official told us, "We give [centers] a certain amount of money, and then we're able to say you have to meet this performance level . . . if you're a center that takes public dollars, you're now subject to academic approval. . . . All programs are measured and all programs are accountable. No other state has this in place."

While the rating system was officially launched in the 2015–2016 school year, its rollout required considerable planning. State officials explained in our interviews that they had researched numerous quality rating systems from around the country and in the end decided on a streamlined approach relying on a single measure, the Classroom Assessment Scoring System (CLASS) (Pianta, La Paro, and Hamre, 2008). CLASS is a common classroom observation measure used in ECE programs across states, and LDOE uses the assessments for both toddler and preschool classrooms.[3] Research suggests that CLASS scores are predictive of children's academic and social development (La Paro, Williamson, and Hatfield, 2014; Sabol et al., 2013). A research study of a 2014–2015 CLASS pilot in five Louisiana parishes indicated that higher CLASS total scores were predictive of pre-K children's developmental gains (Vitiello et al., 2016).[4] That study also provided support for Louisiana's decision to use the total score rather than thresholds for each separate domain to determine the center rating.

In addition to providing LDOE and centers with information about their relative performance on constructs related to teaching and learning, another goal of public access to ratings is to provide families with information about the quality level of centers as they are choosing care for their children. As one official explained, "The number one

---

[3]   An infant classroom CLASS observation is also available and under consideration by LDOE for future use.

[4]   Louisiana is divided into 64 parishes, just as most other states in the United States are organized by county. In ECE, there is generally one ECE network agency for every parish, and there is also typically one school district for every parish.

Key Accountability Indicators for Early Childhood Education

The rating for each publicly funded ECE center is based on an overall score that is based on a seven-point scale averaged across CLASS domains, and this score is presented in a performance profile for each site. Louisiana centers are assigned a site-level rating on a four-level scale: Unsatisfactory, Approaching Proficient, Proficient, or Excellent. This overall rating is presented in the profile alongside separate individual domain scores for classroom quality (for pre-K: emotional support, classroom organization, and instructional support; for toddlers: emotional and behavioral support and engaged support for learning). The profile also includes a few additional pieces of center information that are labeled "use of best practices": use of child assessments, children per teacher, curriculum quality, and prepared teachers (i.e., percentages of teachers with different degree levels and percentage of teachers with a Louisiana teacher certification). The performance profile is posted on the LDOE website and available to the public, and it is incorporated into the Louisiana School Finder website, which provides public information on K–12 (kindergarten through 12th grade) schools.[1] Centers with low ratings over a two-year period will be subject to loss of license or public funding.

---

[1]   Further details of the performance profiles and CLASS observations, including the additional aggregated performance profile generated for each community network, are available through the LDOE website (www.louisianabelieves.com). The School Finder is available at www.louisianaschools.com.

goal is to make sure that we are generating performance profiles that accurately reflect the quality of each early childhood site while also communicating clearly to families information that's useful to them." LDOE officials acknowledged that the performance profile is not a comprehensive definition of ECE quality, nor does it measure fully the best practices for ECE, but the benefit of the simple rating system is that it can be clearly communicated to create a shared vision for what ECE staff and families should expect for classroom quality. Furthermore, it establishes a definition of quality that can be further supported through aligned curriculum, formative child assessments, and professional development and training of ECE staff, including center directors. The compromise in using a single measure, according to our discussions with officials, is that starting with a simple rating system generates shared discussions of what quality looks like and alignment of several LDOE quality improvement initiatives around a common framework. Further refinement of the rating system can occur in the future as centers become more familiar with the system and average quality rises.

This is a high-stakes rating with associated consequences; a center that receives a rating of Unsatisfactory for two consecutive years is subject to a loss of license or public funding. However, the rating system was rolled out in a practice year in 2015–2016 to allow centers to experience the new system and gain information about their quality levels with no consequences before the ratings became high-stakes. One official noted, "One of the best things about doing a practice year and having practice results was that there was less pressure on it. . . . We did calls with everyone, we did webinars, we didn't actually put the results out there in the public until December. We learned a lot from that release." Financial incentives were not aligned with ratings until after the practice year.

The first rating year to count toward license and funding ramifications was the 2016–2017 school year, and those public ratings were released in November 2017 (LDOE, 2017e), although it is too early to know how they might affect family choices. Approximately 1 percent of centers received Unsatisfactory ratings in the first year, and LDOE has targeted those centers for support to focus on quality improvements. On a positive note, officials also indicated that from the practice year to the 2016–2017 ratings, the median CLASS total score increased, indicating that the new rating system could be stimulating some improvements to ECE classrooms.

Local community networks, which are described in further detail later in this chapter, have responsibility to coordinate the CLASS observations for the rating system. Lead agencies for each network are required to adhere to several minimum local protocol requirements, including minimum qualifications for observer training, calibration exercises, number of scoring cycles, and frequency of observations.[5] But a state official noted that there is "a lot of local choice around how . . . to handle local CLASS observations."

Additionally, LDOE contracts with third-party observers to independently observe at least 50 percent of all classrooms within each site each year. Classrooms are selected randomly and include at least one pre-K and one toddler classroom, as appropriate (LDOE, undated-m). If scores of third-party versus local network observers differ by more than one point within a domain, the third-party scores are used for the rating. These additional observers can also be used to assess sites where LDOE staff have noticed very low or very high scores or have other questions about observer accuracy in the course of ongoing monitoring of data. The Vitiello and colleagues (2016) study of the pilot observations suggested that local network observers may score higher than independent observers and that the use of third-party observers could help ensure reliability. One interview respondent noted that although the third-party observers serve as a quality check for the observation scoring to ensure a reliable system across programs, the intent is that the local community will have primary responsibility for observations, adding:

> [O]ne of the biggest reasons we built a system that has both local and third-party observations is because we wanted to build local capacity around those CLASS tools. We wanted to make sure that the people who were supposed to be supporting and leading—like school leaders and center directors— . . . actually understood what early childhood quality was. . . . The fact that even the center directors know how to talk [about CLASS observations] is a really big deal. So yes, there are concerns about local accuracy, bias. . . . That's why we have the third-party contract, that's why we do the replacements, that's why we do the analysis in the course of the year, look for red flags. But we think that

---

[5]   Guidance is provided to networks, such as the "Local Protocol for CLASS Observations" worksheet distributed by LDOE.

trade-off is worth it, because we're building this understanding of what early childhood quality should look like.

Action 2. Strengthen lead teacher preparation requirements through a new ECE teacher credential: the Early Childhood Ancillary Certificate.

One important approach for improving classroom quality and child outcomes is to ensure that center teaching staff have minimum preparation levels that include early childhood knowledge and experiences. Louisiana has taken the step of creating and supporting a new teacher credential, the Early Childhood Ancillary Certificate, which will be required for all lead teachers in Louisiana's Type III publicly funded centers starting in 2019.[6] This certificate establishes a minimum level of preparation teachers must have, which is based on the national Child Development Associate (CDA) credential, which requires 120 hours of training with at least ten hours in each of eight subject areas, as well as applied practice experiences in addition to coursework (LDOE, undated-b). Teachers can attain the Early Childhood Ancillary Certificate through completion of the CDA. Additionally, the certificate is part of a broader career pathway for all ECE professionals and will be linked to the new Louisiana Birth-to-Kindergarten bachelor's program for teacher credentialing. It is also aligned with the regional ECE graduation pathways discussed further in Chapter Four. The Early Childhood Ancillary Certificate contributes to the effort to unify the ECE system and foster a professionalized workforce (LDOE, undated-b).

Toward this goal of a prepared workforce, LDOE is supporting the creation of BESE-approved Early Childhood Ancillary Certificate programs to meet the CDA training requirements for teachers without certification. Starting in July 2018, teachers without certification who are pursuing the Early Childhood Ancillary Certificate through attainment of the CDA are required to earn it from BESE-approved programs, which go beyond CDA training requirements to include coursework-connected practice. Through the LDOE Believe and Pre-

---

[6]   A lead teacher is present in each ECE classroom and has primary responsibility for the classroom's activities.

pare Early Childhood program,[7] "Louisiana has established a process to evaluate and approve teacher preparation programs that are preparing child care teachers for the Early Childhood Ancillary Certificate" (LDOE, undated-b). LDOE provides start-up grants and technical assistance to entities (e.g., resource and referral agencies, higher education, high schools, and professional development companies) that apply to become approved Early Childhood Ancillary Certificate programs. The rollout of these new programs starting in 2015 occurred through an initial pilot of four programs, and lessons learned from that pilot led to some additional program changes. Fourteen programs have been approved as of January 2018. In April 2018, the state approved a vendor to operate a statewide online Early Childhood Ancillary Certificate program.

Aligned Resources

LDOE has also worked to implement Louisiana's ECE vision through provision of aligned resources designed to create and promote a shared sense of understanding of ECE quality, particularly for Type III centers mandated to participate in the rating system.

> **Action 3.** Signal to ECE staff which curricula, formative assessments, and professional development are high-quality and standards-aligned.

As in the K–12 sector, use of high-quality curricula that are linked to performance standards is perceived by LDOE officials to be an important component of providing high-quality instruction in early childhood classrooms. The new performance profiles for early childhood centers include a self-reported measure of curriculum use as an additional indicator by which parents can judge centers. LDOE created the Child Care Curriculum Initiative (LDOE, 2016a) in 2016–2017 to incentivize the use of curricula that have been judged as high-

---

[7] This program is the early childhood version of Louisiana's Believe and Prepare program, discussed in Chapter Three.

quality by a panel of LDOE staff and teacher reviewers, rated from Tier I (exemplifies highest quality) to Tier III (limited quality). This early childhood curricula review process is very similar to that used for grades K–12, described in further detail in the next chapter. The state supports annotated reviews of infant, toddler, and preschool curricula, which are available online for easy access by early childhood educators. All curricula rated Tier I are considered to be consistent with the *Louisiana Birth to Five Early Learning and Development Standards*, which were developed in 2013 in response to Act 3 requirements and outline a continuum of developmental milestones in support of the state's definition of kindergarten readiness (LDOE, 2013b). Furthermore, resource and referral agencies provide centers with training and coaching for implementing Tier I high-quality curricula.

It is unclear to what extent centers used any type of curriculum before this initiative started in 2016–2017, and although sites self-report curricula for the performance profiles, it remains unclear how much the adopted curricula are consistently used with fidelity in classrooms. Nonetheless, the Child Care Curriculum Initiative is perceived by LDOE officials to be an important first step in signaling the value of high-quality ECE curricula to help improve classroom quality and meet rating requirements. LDOE is also incentivizing curriculum adoption through monetary incentives (see below). A future step for Louisiana will be to gauge and monitor actual curriculum use and its relationship with performance ratings.

Along with curriculum, LDOE is also recommending and supporting the use of Teaching Strategies GOLD™ for child assessment (state pays for all publicly funded children), including an online entry system for GOLD data (LDOE, 2016c). This assessment is aligned with elements of Tier I curricula and the measures captured by the CLASS (LDOE, 2016c). Moreover, professional development for ECE staff is aimed toward providing classroom supports aligned with CLASS measures (e.g., using Child Care and Development Fund monies for this type of aligned training related to quality improvement) (LDOE, 2017c).

As these initiatives were piloted, LDOE provided financial support for training on standards, assessments, and CLASS. Furthermore, as one state official noted, LDOE worked closely with Head Start to ensure that LDOE's supports were standards-aligned and that LDOE efforts did not put Head Start centers at odds with their federal requirements.

Incentives

In addition to resources, Louisiana has provided several incentives through the funding initiatives described below to support ECE quality improvement in the context of the rating system and to provide families with improved access to high-quality choices.

> **Action 4.** Increase funding for CCAP subsidies to increase parity and encourage diversity in types of centers serving publicly funded children.

One issue that Louisiana sought to address was the funding disparity for children enrolling in different types of centers, specifically pre-K centers funded through LDOE and child care centers funded through CCAP subsidies. CCAP provides financial assistance to low-income families for child care costs. Families who apply for CCAP must meet several requirements: They must be financially responsible for the child care of children under 13 (or children with disabilities under 18); their income must be below a certain threshold (for instance, for a three-person household to be eligible for CCAP in 2017, its members must collectively make $2,684 or less per month); and every adult in the household must work or attend school or training programs (LDOE, undated-r; LDOE, 2017r).

During our interviews in fall 2017, state officials explained that if LDOE were to require that all centers meet the same performance standards through the rating system, then they should have comparable funding at the center level to meet performance standards, regardless of funding source. Previously, the CCAP amount provided for a family was $1,282, which was just 28 percent of the amount provided for a family in a pre-K program (LDOE, 2015a). To address these disparities, in 2015, BESE approved changes that allowed Louisiana to increase the

CCAP rates for providers to nearly $4,000 per family annually and to loosen the eligibility requirements for the CCAP program to increase access (LDOE, 2015a). Specifically, "We tried to create parity between private and public pre-K subsidy," according to one LDOE official. The state also reduced the co-pays required of families, changed the family subsidy eligibility based on working hours, and increased the family eligibility period so that more families would have similar access to all types of publicly funded centers.

Additionally, before 2017, the CCAP program required all adults in the household to work 30 hours or more per week or attend school. Now, households are eligible for CCAP if adults in the household work 20 hours or more per week, or at least 15 hours per week in the case of families with children who have disabilities (given the additional challenges faced by such families). Also, students enrolled in education or training programs full-time are now eligible for CCAP funds (LDOE, 2017s). As a result of these changes, participation increased. One significant consequence of this rate increase and eligibility expansion, however, was a CCAP waitlist starting in July 2017, when CCAP funds were exhausted.

Another issue the state sought to address related to parity was the types of centers that publicly funded children could access. In 2014, LDOE was awarded a federal Preschool Development Expansion Grant based in part on taking advantage of the new ECE community network structure and the ability to offer additional pre-K slots for four-year-olds in child care centers in high-need communities. The grant is expected to provide about 4,600 new slots over four years starting in the 2015–2016 school year, with families able to choose among diverse settings including child care, public and nonpublic schools, and Head Start (LDOE, undated-o). The state will also use these grant funds to improve quality among existing centers serving about 6,000 children. This effort seeks to diversify the pre-K delivery settings in communities and raise quality in child care settings. As explained by one state official, these new pre-K slots are funded at a higher rate than typical child care slots and may help raise the overall performance of the center. Specifically, these pre-K slots will be funded at about $5,185 per child (LDOE, undated-o).

In addition to using funds from the expansion grant to add slots in child care centers, the state uses funding from the existing Nonpublic Schools Early Childhood Development (NSECD) program. NSECD provides subsidies to low-income four-year-olds whose families meet eligibility guidelines for Temporary Assistance for Needy Families. Classrooms supported by NSECD include both NSECD-funded children and children funded through other sources (LDOE, undated-p).

Action 5. Provide funding incentives tied to higher quality ratings, teacher training, and curriculum use.

To further incentivize higher quality, Louisiana allocated funding tied to performance profile ratings and teachers' attainment of an Early Childhood Ancillary Certificate. First, the state added funding to strengthen its School Readiness Tax Credits to reward teachers with certification who stay in the ECE field and to reward higher program ratings. Several different stakeholder groups are eligible for these innovative tax credits,[8] which have received national attention in recent years. According to LDOE (2017a), recent tax credit increases mean teachers are eligible to earn higher credits based on earning an Early Childhood Ancillary Certificate and documenting retention in the ECE field; starting in 2018, this could total up to about $3,300 per year for Type III teachers. Center directors will also receive credits based on site performance measured by program ratings. Moreover, the state also increased its CCAP bonuses for providers by 3 percent to support quality improvements. However, centers with lower ratings will, over time, become ineligible for CCAP bonuses, a policy that is intended to incentivize them to raise their quality (LDOE, 2017a).

---

[8]   Credits are available for the following groups: (1) ECE directors and staff working at least six months in a center participating in the rating system and enrolled in the career pathways system; (2) ECE providers who enroll foster children or children participating in CCAP; (3) taxpayers with a dependent under age six who attended a center receiving two or more stars, with higher credits for higher ratings; (4) businesses providing specific types of support to centers participating in the ratings system; and (5) businesses making donations to child care resource and referral agencies. For more detail, see Louisiana Department of Revenue (undated).

Families are also eligible for state tax credits based on the quality rating of the center that their children attend.

Second, Louisiana provides funding for teacher tuition scholarships so that completing the training for the Early Childhood Ancillary Certificate in approved preparation programs can be done for little to no out-of-pocket costs (LDOE, undated-b). Additionally, Believe and Prepare Early Childhood grantees are eligible to receive funding up to $30,000 to start up an Ancillary Certificate program (LDOE, undated-b). Lastly, a feature of the Child Care Curriculum Initiative is that LDOE will reimburse 80 percent of a center's cost to purchase Tier I curricula (LDOE, 2016a), and officials noted that network lead agencies may cover the remaining 20 percent to make the center's curriculum purchase no or low cost.

Communication and Planning Processes

LDOE has strived to provide clear and consistent messages about ECE mandates, resources, and incentives to stakeholders while planning, piloting, and rolling out new initiatives. These activities include the ongoing LDOE communications highlighted in Chapter One. That said, the creation and structure of the community network system and lead agencies are unique to ECE. These structures are used for planning, administration, and communication purposes.

> **Action 6.** Define and require community networks for administration and communication, including coordinated ECE program enrollment for families.

Community networks are required under Act 3 through a mandate for the creation of a statewide Early Childhood Care and Education Network (ECEN). In Act 3 language, the ECEN is intended to be "a comprehensive and integrated network through which to manage and oversee all programs funded through state or federal resources" that provide ECE services. Today, ECEN comprises 65 lead agencies for community networks through which planning and coordination occurs at the local level, representing all 64 Louisiana parishes. Lead agencies have three primary requirements for funding receipt, as per their contract with LDOE: (1) Conduct administrative functions for the network such as community partner engagement and serving as fiscal agent; (2) coordinate CLASS observations twice annually for every center in the network (described earlier); and (3) lead coordinated enrollment efforts for birth to age five programs in the network (LDOE, 2016c).

These networks are perceived by state officials we spoke with as critical for successful communication about quality and access between the state, local communities, providers, and families. Dedicated LDOE staff interact with the networks and provide communication channels, and they listen for feedback and lessons learned. The information LDOE gathers from networks is then shared with the LDOE Early Childhood Office in regular meetings. One official summed up that "broad communication with various stakeholders is our most effective lever, and hearing their concerns, not just providing them information but having a true two-way communication process, has served us well. Because in the end it's all about relationships and keeping people focused on the ultimate outcome, which is the benefit for children and families."

According to the state officials with whom we spoke, these networks have been very important as the state has developed new policies in response to Act 3. For example, the networks themselves were piloted with 13 local networks in 2013, and, from that pilot, experiences were shared and momentum built so that all centers were represented by a local network within three years. One state official put it this way:

> We decided the best way to do this would be to identify champions, to clearly develop our concept as best we could, and have people sign on as champions of that concept and then on an opt-in basis, ask folks to come on board and let us see what implementation looked like locally. Because that's where the rubber meets the road.

Moreover, the state pilot of the CLASS observations, and the practice year in 2015–2016, provided useful feedback from communities and networks. That feedback and practice was key to gaining provider acceptance for the process and identifying areas in need of change before the full rollout and accountability implications in the 2016–2017 school year. The lead agencies are perceived by officials as playing a critical role in helping the state create clear communication strategies for rolling out initiatives, such as performance profiles, that reinforce center quality expectations.

LDOE officials often referred in our interviews to the key goals of ECE quality and access. Quality is institutionalized in the performance profiles, and the access piece is achieved primarily through the networks' coordinated enrollment efforts, required by BESE Bulletin 140. Local community networks are tasked with implementing coordinated enrollment for all publicly funded programs in their network as one key aspect of a unified ECE system. When it is fully implemented, the process will allow families to identify all available ECE seats and what they qualify for, submit one enrollment application and indicate their preferences for centers, and then be matched to their preferred centers using a rank ordering system and matching based on available spaces (LDOE, 2017a).

The network lead agencies guidebook (LDOE, 2016c) specifies that networks collaborate with all program partners to identify ECE spaces, determine an eligibility process that informs families of the programs for which they can apply, and use a common application form that allows families to rank their program preferences. They should also work with local resource and referral agencies to communicate this process to families so they have easy access to the application and maintain a waitlist coordinated across all programs.

The coordinated enrollment is not fully developed in each network yet, so it is still a work in progress and locally determined, with each network having autonomy to a great degree over how it functions. One potential concern going forward is programs' resistance to change in enrollment procedures, as explained by one official: "People care about enrollment, it's what their funding is tied to. Enrollment is complicated, and if you have a process that works, you don't want to change that."

Although coordinated enrollment processes are locally determined, LDOE has provided technical assistance to community networks. One official noted that

> For a long time once we launched coordinated enrollment, it was about pushing models into the field, and that has been pretty successful. We have a number of communities using technology that have learned from each other in the process. . . . So building on the exemplars has been pretty successful. The next phase is identifying . . . concerns and how we in the department should be mitigating that.

Finally, another communication tool that has helped LDOE create clear messaging on a shared vision of quality and how centers play a role are the two LDOE guidebooks related to ECE. The first, *Guide to Success for Early Childhood Community Network Lead Agencies* (LDOE, 2016c), reinforces the three primary lead agency requirements. The second, *Louisiana's Pre–K Through Third Grade Guidebook for Sites and System Leaders* (LDOE, 2017b), outlines five key state strategies, such as implementing high-quality curricula, and focuses on the continuum of learning across grades. Both guidebooks were discussed in detail with network staff during the Supervisor Collaboration quarterly meeting we observed in fall 2017.

Potential Implementation Challenges

Louisiana has undertaken rapid changes in ECE policies over the past five years, and the next stage, as expressed by various state officials, is to continue to provide supports, monitor progress, and modify policies and initiatives in response to implementation successes and challenges. Among the challenges remaining are equitable access to high-quality centers, statewide consensus on the value of the performance profile ratings, ability to support the Early Childhood Ancillary Certificate system for all teachers, and adoption and use of Tier I curricula.

Equitable Access and Opportunity for High-Quality Early Childhood Education

An ongoing implementation challenge will be to provide families with reliable and accessible information on center quality ratings that they may use to make better-informed child care decisions, while also ensuring that families have equitable access to high-quality centers across the state. This may be especially important in select geographic regions, such as rural areas that may have a more limited selection of centers and trained staff. The state seeks to provide a more seamless experience for providers and families that is focused on the shared goal of ensuring that all children enter kindergarten ready. As part of that goal, Louisiana would ideally want more families ultimately choosing to enroll their children in centers that are rated proficient or above. Yet this also raises the concern about systematically connecting quality and access for families, especially through the local network structures families have developed and with limited state funding for subsidies. For instance, by increasing the CCAP rates to incentivize centers' quality improvement efforts, the state has exhausted available funding before meeting the child care needs of all eligible low-income families. Families may recognize high quality but not be able to afford it. As another example, one state official noted a concern about how the state will handle future license revocations for consistently low-performing centers if those centers are located in areas where families already face very limited options for child care. Families may not have full access to quality in their community in the short term. Quality and access are goals that must be balanced as the quality improvement system develops. Moreover, child care is a private market, and some aspects of supply of and demand for quality may be outside the control of local networks or LDOE.

On a related note, whether all families have access and opportunity to receive high-quality ECE relates to the extent to which ECE centers are able to improve the quality of the care they provide. While some ECE centers may serve as exemplars for high-quality child care, it is difficult to know whether all—or even most centers—have the capacity and support to reach the same level of quality and what it might cost to get them to that level. Measuring and understanding the cost involved in quality improvement, and how much improvement is realistically feasible, will be ongoing challenges for LDOE.

Consensus of Value of Rating System

As the performance profiles roll out, Louisiana will need to continue communication to ensure that ECE providers perceive that the quality ratings accurately measure key factors related to improving quality and that these ratings are applied consistently across centers without undue burden to programs. One method will be to continue to monitor and support local networks in public communications about quality ratings. It is expected that some centers will begin to express concerns about the rating system when bonuses or family perceptions are affected by lower-than-expected ratings. A focus for the state in the immediate future is managing the public perception of the rating system and providing clear messages about why ratings related to improved child outcomes are necessary. One official also noted that the state will examine the thresholds for rating levels and may make adjustments to raise the bar to better signal proficient levels as the system matures. To provide support for the rating system in general, and to make any needed refinements, the state will require that child outcome data be linked to center enrollment, and LDOE will need to analyze the relationships between ratings based on the CLASS measure and outcomes over time to make sure the system is improving kindergarten readiness as intended. If outcomes are not related to higher CLASS scores as expected, the state may need to rethink use of the CLASS as a strong quality signal, or consider how to make adjustments to improve reliability and validity of the ratings.

Capacity to Provide Early Childhood Ancillary Certificates

A further state challenge is making sure that all ECE lead teachers are able to enroll in programs that will allow them to receive Early Childhood Ancillary Certificates by 2019 and that new lead teachers can do so annually thereafter. The state appears to be on track to achieve statewide capacity to enroll teachers who wish to pursue the Early Childhood Ancillary Certificate, according to interviewees, but doing so requires ramping up the number of approved teacher preparation programs and state support for scholarships and grantee start-up costs. The addition of an online program option, under development, will be helpful to reach some teachers who may not have ready access to the existing preparation programs. In addition to capacity issues, an implementation concern for the state is assessing the quality of the new preparation programs on an ongoing basis to ensure that teachers are being trained as intended (e.g., in a manner consistent with Louisiana's Birth to Five standards). A state official noted that LDOE is developing an accountability framework for teacher preparation programs to measure the impact of these investments.

Use of and High-Quality Support for Tier I Curricula

A final challenge will be the continued communication, support, and incentives to encourage all centers to adopt Tier I curricula to improve instruction. The state has created the reviewed list of curricula that is publicly available and signals what LDOE and teacher experts consider high-quality, and the Child Care Curriculum Initiative provides financial incentives for curriculum adoption. These are important initial steps, and the self-reporting of curriculum use on the performance profiles will provide some evidence of the success of these efforts over time. Beyond adoption, it will also be important to monitor how well the curricula are used in daily classroom practices, how teachers are supported through aligned professional development opportunities to use the curricula as intended, and, ultimately, how teacher-child interactions are improved as a result of high-quality curricula.

In subsequent research that is part of our larger study, we plan to talk with ECE network leads, directors, and teachers in multiple contexts to learn more about the challenges they face and how the LDOE has supported their work. We will also try to understand more about the state's capacity to support teachers' pursuit of Early Childhood Ancillary Certificates, and networks' governance capacity to sustain ongoing efforts at the local level.

CHAPTER THREE

The K–12 Academics and Teacher Preparation

Over the past decade, Louisiana K–12 public schools have faced numerous challenges. Louisiana is one of the poorest states in the nation and—according to an *Education Week* report—spent less on education than 36 other U.S. states as recently as 2013 (Education Week Research Center, 2016). Since the National Assessment of Educational Progress (NAEP) was first administered in 1992, students' NAEP scores have been significantly lower than national averages in every tested subject (The Nation's Report Card, undated-a). However, as noted in Chapter One, Louisiana students have made considerable gains on the ACT over the past few years, as well as some other student outcomes measures.[1] In a prior RAND report (Kaufman, Thompson, and Opfer, 2016), we highlighted some differences between K–12 teachers in Louisiana and teachers in other states, based on data from the RAND American Teacher Panel. Louisiana teachers were more likely than other U.S. teachers to know which reading approaches and mathematics content were well aligned with their state standards. In addition, a large majority of Louisiana teachers—more than 70 percent—were using Eureka Math for their mathematics instruction, despite the fact

---

[1] In 2015, fourth-grade students' average scores for reading on the NAEP rose significantly and increased more than scores of students in any other state. Fourth-grade students' scores in mathematics also rose, though not significantly. However, in 2017, fourth-grade students' scores decreased significantly in both reading and math. Some evidence suggests that the significant decrease in students' scores might be attributable to students who took NAEP online for the first time (Bjorklund-Young and Steiner, 2018). See The Nation's Report Card state profiles (undated-b) for more information on Louisiana students' performance on the NAEP.

that parish school districts are not required by the state to adopt any particular curricula.

The 2016 RAND report linked Louisiana teachers' higher knowledge and uptake of Eureka Math—compared with other U.S. teachers—to a handful of LDOE strategies, including an academic strategy focused on integration and alignment among systems supporting state standards, transparent and regular communication about academics with stakeholders across the U.S. system, and strong support for local decisionmaking. In this chapter, we attempt to unpack those strategies further. We particularly consider how LDOE has utilized mandates, resources, incentives, and communication/planning strategies to support its K–12 goals in specific content areas.

This chapter highlights the central role of curriculum in LDOE's theory of implementation about how to support high-quality teaching and learning. We specifically discuss how LDOE started with federally required and state-mandated K–12 standards and assessments in key content areas as a definition and goal for quality, as other states have done. But what has separated Louisiana from other states, according to our analysis, was LDOE's work to support and incentivize use of resources and tools closely aligned with state standards. This work echoes similar work that took place simultaneously in ECE to support access to high-quality, standards-aligned curricula, professional development, and formative assessments. Louisiana's textbook policy does not require use of any curricula, but—as also in ECE—it does set forth a process for LDOE to conduct ongoing, rigorous reviews of instructional materials for alignment of materials to state standards, and it also grants district state contracts for less expensive purchase of materials that LDOE reviewers have defined as high-quality. LDOE has also worked with vendors and experts to develop and/or recommend both formative assessments and professional development closely aligned with recommended curricula.

Our chapter combines overview of K–12 goals and actions with goals and actions related to teacher preparation. As state policies have focused more on educator effectiveness in recent years, teacher preparation has received more attention from state policymakers. The National Council on Teacher Quality (NCTQ) summarizes state policies related to teacher preparation on a regular basis, and they have noted state progress in setting minimum GPA and performance thresholds for teacher candidates, although several states do not require a test to gauge academic aptitude of teacher candidates (NCTQ, 2017). In addition, NCTQ (2017) has noted that a handful of states collect and report on data connecting teacher preparation program graduates to district-level hiring statistics.[2]

In Louisiana, LDOE's teacher preparation work particularly mirrors the intended theory of implementation we highlighted in Chapter One. First, state officials did a lot of information-gathering to understand the current state of teacher preparation and teacher needs within school districts by surveying directors of teacher preparation programs, as well as current teachers and principals. As also discussed later in this chapter, survey results suggested inadequate opportunities for teacher trainees to engage in hands-on student teaching in classrooms, as well as the need for better coordination and collaboration between districts and preparation providers. A subsequent LDOE report (2014a) summarized the survey results and salient challenges for teacher preparation, as well as ideas beginning to percolate through piloting of partnerships between teacher preparation programs and school districts within the state. In spring 2015, LDOE followed up on the momentum created through the survey report to hold a policy forum on teacher preparation with legislators, educators, K–12 and higher education leaders, and members of BESE. During the forum, LDOE shared its policy proposals for teacher preparation, which were followed by further funding to districts to partner with teacher preparation organizations and "test out" competencies and yearlong residencies. This work established buy-in that provided more support for mandated requirements, which were passed into policy by BESE in 2016.

---

[2] While NCTQ lauded Louisiana for connecting program graduates' student growth data to its teacher preparation program, NCTQ also noted that Louisiana had not connected program completion with district hiring statistics.

Key Goals and Actions

> [The Army] used these huge elaborate battle plans . . . but inevitably they would go into battle, and they would fall apart. So they came up with this idea of "Commander's Intent," which was basically: at the end of the day, you need to get the flag on the top of the hill. . . . When it came to battle time, they had drilled so much that 'you get the flag to the top of the hill,' that the soldiers could make decisions around that goal. . . . So we've kind of applied that same theory to education.

This quotation, from an LDOE official, was inspired by the idea of "Commander's Intent" in *Made to Stick*, by Chip and Dan Heath (2007). The LDOE official elaborated:

> If we can come up with what is our "Commander's Intent" for English language arts (ELA), social studies, or whatever content area, we can help people understand the various ways they might accomplish that. But, at the end of the day, we're all marching in the same direction, or working toward the same goal.

In K–12 core subject areas (mathematics, ELA, science, and social studies), LDOE has leveraged recently revised, more-rigorous standards to provide clear goals for what constitutes high-quality student work. Perhaps more importantly, LDOE has done considerable work to integrate and align instructional resources with the goal and definition of quality set by standards, as well as put forth a set of mandates and incentives that encourage use of those resources.

Through the Elementary and Secondary Education Act—reauthorized recently as the Every Student Succeeds Act (ESSA)—the federal government has long required all U.S. states to have K–12 academic standards for core subjects that specify key content that students should be expected to learn. With the advent of the Common Core State Standards, Louisiana—like most states—adopted new standards for mathematics and ELA that highlight content and goals for classroom instruction adapted from the Common Core (Achieve, 2017; Korn, Gamboa, and Polikoff, 2016; Norton, Ash and Ballinger, 2017). For example, as noted by Achieve (2017), most recent state mathematics standards documents focus somewhat on the idea of "balancing" a focus on procedural skills and fluency with a focus on conceptual understanding and the application of mathematics to real-world examples and problems. Most states also emphasize students' engagement in "practice standards"—such as making sense of problems and modeling with mathematics—that the National Council for Teachers of Mathematics has emphasized as an integral part of mathematics instruction. Also as noted by Achieve (2017), in ELA, most states emphasize close reading of grade-level and complex texts, although the guidance states give in regard to text complexity might vary somewhat.

Interviews with state officials who focus on K–12 academics emphasized goals for classroom instruction that were closely aligned with state standards documents. For example, for English language arts, a state official described the goal as "all students are able to read, understand, and express their understanding of complex, grade-level texts." That goal is also highlighted at the beginning of a public document on Louisiana's ELA standards (LDOE, 2016d). For mathematics, another LDOE state official noted,

> I am really looking for three things [in the classroom] and we actually train principals to walk into classrooms and ask themselves three questions. The first one . . . is what the students are doing aligned to the standards? And we tell them, if they're using the Eureka curriculum, and I mean using it, I don't mean like putting it over in the corner, then you can assume that answer is yes.

That state official continued by noting that she looks for evidence that kids are "doing the math" and "talking about the math." Both activities are emphasized in standards documents on supporting students' conceptual understanding of mathematics and supporting students to make sense of problems and reason mathematically (LDOE, 2017f).

For science and social studies, new standards have been developed relatively recently. New science standards focus on three key shifts that are also reflected in the Next Generation Science Standards (Next Generation Science Standards, undated): application of content knowledge to scientific phenomenon; being able to investigate, evaluate, and reason scientifically; and being able to connect ideas across scientific disciplines (LDOE, undated-c). A state official with whom we spoke discussed the key shifts the state wants to see for social studies: that students use sources to regularly learn content; make connections among people, places, ideas, and events across time and place; and express informed opinions.

To meet the goals addressed by state standards in core content areas, LDOE has engaged in several key actions aimed at preparing strong educators and supporting their instruction in schools and classrooms (Table 3.1).

The policy levers invoked to support these actions include mandates related to federal requirements, textbook review policies, and teacher preparation program requirements. In addition, LDOE staff

Table 3.1
K–12 System and Teacher Preparation Actions in Louisiana

Action	Policy Lever
1. Use state standards, assessments, and accountability to define and communicate a high bar for what is expected from schools and students.	Mandate: ESSA
2. Codify a vision for high-quality teacher preparation that includes clear requirements and accountability structures for teacher preparation programs.	Mandate
3. Signal to educators which instructional materials—including curricula and assessments—are high-quality and which are not.	Resource alignment
4. Increase the supply of high-quality, curriculum-specific professional development options, and provide clear information about those options.	Resource alignment
5. Provide funding incentives tied to use of high-quality curricula, professional development, and formative assessments.	Incentive
6. Incentivize early adoption of the state's vision for high-quality teacher preparation through district-teacher preparation program partnership funding.	Incentive
7. Create communication structures to identify champions and gather information.	Communication and planning processes

focused on K–12 academics talked about development of a suite of aligned resources to support teachers' work with students in the classroom, as well as ensuring clear and frequent communication to districts, schools, and teachers about those resources. While LDOE has incentivized use of these tools, districts are left to make local decisions about what tools and training to use for teaching and learning. For teacher preparation, a significant period of testing and planning preceded BESE policies requiring teacher preparation programs to adopt competencies and establish yearlong residencies.

The timeline for all these actions has been recent. With the exception of Louisiana's adoption of the Common Core in 2010, key actions unfolded starting around 2014. Figure 3.1 highlights the timeline for the main policies and activities that were Louisiana's work for K–12 academics and teacher preparation. At the same time, much of LDOE's aligned resource work is ongoing, including regular reviews of curricula, formative assessments and recommendations for professional development vendors.

Mandates

On their face, mandates are simply "rules governing the actions of individuals and agencies" (McDonnell and Elmore, 1987). Yet, federal and state mandates for standards and tests have also created state accountability systems that are intended to pressure schools and districts to encourage higher student achievement. State officials with whom we spoke acknowledged the importance of accountability systems for emphasizing and encouraging what they value. One state official, for example, said, "I think we have seen over the last few years the impact in districts of what happens when we put something in the accountability system. We see it as a way of saying, this is what we value." Another state official comments that LDOE has "a clear and ambitious accountability system. . . . We work hard to ensure accountability represents and reinforces our vision for what we want students to learn every day." In this section, we discuss key state actions related to mandates. While public reporting is a kind of incentive that supports

Figure 3.1
Timeline for Major Policies and Activities in K–12 Academics and Teacher Preparation

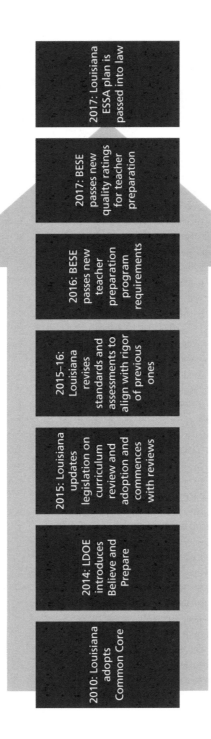

2010: Louisiana adopts Common Core

2014: LDOE introduces Believe and Prepare

2015: Louisiana updates legislation on curriculum review and adoption and commences with reviews

2015–16: Louisiana revises standards and assessments to align with rigor of previous ones

2016: BESE passes new teacher preparation program requirements

2017: BESE passes new quality ratings for teacher preparation

2017: Louisiana ESSA plan is passed into law

RAND RR2303-3.1

Louisiana's accountability system, it is also a federal requirement. We thus also highlight the role of public reporting as part of this section.

Action 1. Use state standards, assessments, and accountability to define and communicate a high bar for what is expected from schools and students.

As noted earlier, ESSA has required all U.S. states to adopt career and college readiness standards, to adopt statewide assessments intended to test mastery of standards, and to provide public reporting of assessment results. Districts, in turn, are required to administer the assessments. Results on assessments have consequences. Federal mandates require states to develop interventions to support improvements in persistently struggling schools with consistently low assessment results.

In Louisiana—as in many other states—the adoption of standards and assessments has been complicated and politically charged. In response to the earlier NCLB legislation and RTTT initiative, Louisiana adopted the Common Core State Standards and also joined the Partnership for Assessment of Readiness for College and Career (PARCC), with the intention to administer the PARCC-developed assessments.[3] However, Louisiana experienced some backlash against the Common Core and PARCC. BESE's adoption of the Common Core State Standards in 2010 drew considerable protests from conservative state legislature members and led to litigation. The standards were revised by Louisiana educators and eventually approved in 2016, although independent sources suggest that the standards retained the high expectations (e.g., use of complex texts and mathematical explanation and reasoning) present in the Common Core (Korn, Gamboa, and Polikoff, 2016). Louisiana students initially participated in the PARCC assessment in 2015. However, in that year Louisiana also passed legislation requiring that fewer questions on the annual standardized state test be drawn from PARCC (Sentell, 2015). In response, LDOE staff collaborated with experts to ensure that the state assessment remained

---

[3]   PARCC was one of two multistate consortia that developed assessments aligned with the Common Core; the Smarter Balanced Assessment Consortium was the other.

well aligned with state standards and also retained the rigor and challenge of items in the original PARCC assessment. Independent assessments have suggested that the Louisiana Educational Assessment Program (LEAP) assessments can be compared to results from PARCC in other states.[4]

State officials did not frequently discuss the role of the Compass leader and teacher evaluation system. Compass is a set of state-approved rubrics through which Louisiana teachers, leaders, and counselors are evaluated (LDOE, 2017q). While Compass and teacher evaluation did not come up much in our conversations with state officials, one official did note that the evaluation system has played an important role in their work:

> The most important part [of Compass] is how it has affected teachers' goals. It has shifted teachers' focus to asking what students should be learning, the standards and the content. I think teachers talk more consistently in a way that is about their responsibility for student outcomes and the specifics of what students should be learning.

At the same time, another official told us that they have "pivoted away from classroom level accountability. . . . It's just not front and center for us. We've leaned into preparing teachers for [accountability policies] rather than first create back-end evaluation systems."

Action 2. Codify a vision for high-quality teacher preparation that includes clear requirements and accountability structures for teacher preparation programs.

For teacher preparation institutions, Louisiana defined a set of requirements intended to better align teacher preparation with K–12 standards and goals. However, those requirements were passed by BESE (which has authority over teacher preparation program requirements in Louisiana) after a few years of information gathering, plan-

---

[4]   See DePascale (2017).

ning, and LDOE funding for district-teacher preparation partnerships that tested out the requirements before they were passed into policy. Furthermore, the teacher preparation requirements passed by BESE have been instituted gradually. LDOE started out in 2014 asking for the changes among preparation providers participating in pilot partnerships, with the requirements to be put in place by July 2018 in all institutions. In this section—which focuses on mandates as a policy lever for change—we describe the requirements that were originally defined by LDOE and passed into policy in 2016. In later sections, we describe the incentives, communication, and planning that supported these requirements.

LDOE has defined three key components that define the design of quality teacher preparation in Louisiana: a yearlong residency requirement, a competency-based curriculum requirement, and a partnership model intended to strengthen the relationships between teacher preparation programs and the school districts that hire their graduates. To enact this definition for teacher preparation design into policy, LDOE leveraged the regulatory authority of BESE. BESE approves teacher preparation providers and sets the criteria for that approval process. In the words of one state official: "[O]ur state education board has really broad, significant regulatory authority with respect to teacher preparation, which . . . really was underutilized [prior to the current administration]."

In October 2016, after two years of research and piloting, BESE passed the LDOE's three policy priorities—competencies, residencies, and partnerships—into policy. These regulations require teacher preparation programs to provide teacher candidates with a yearlong teaching residency under the supervision of a mentor teacher and to offer connected, competency-based coursework that helps teachers develop professional skills they will need in the classroom. The regulations also encourage partnerships between preparation providers and districts by setting expectations for collaboration between those two entities. These policies go into full effect in 2018–2019; any teacher candidate admitted to a program after July 1, 2018, is required to have access to these new program components (LDOE, 2017g).

Key Accountability Indicators for K–12 Academics and Teacher Preparation

As noted in Chapter One, Louisiana's ESSA plan raised the bar for what counts as an "A" within this letter grade system, requiring both higher student scores on assessments and higher high school graduation rates than what was required previously. Louisiana's ESSA plan also includes a new growth index, which includes yearly growth targets for students who do not achieve mastery and compares students who have not met growth targets to similar peers. In addition, a new indicator signaling how a school is providing opportunities such as Advanced Placement (AP) courses and extracurricular activities for students will count as 5 percent of a school's letter grade.

All of these indicators have been newly incorporated into Louisiana's public reporting to incentivize accountability. Louisiana has long provided public report cards for schools and districts. Report cards profile schools and assign letter grades based on a set of key indicators. However, the newest online iteration of these public report cards integrates videos and pop-up text boxes to describe different measures, and the interactive report cards provide figures illustrating student mastery of grade level content, progress over time, progress in each core subject, and gaps among subgroups. More information on high school report cards is included in the next chapter. But high school report cards include both college and career ready indicators, as well as graduation rates and a new "quality of graduation" indicator.[1]

Schools that receive an overall or subgroup rating of a "D" or "F" for two consecutive years or more are labeled as requiring either urgent or comprehensive intervention; such schools are required to submit a plan indicating what intervention(s) they plan to pursue,

---

[1]   Report cards are publicly available online at the Louisiana School Finder website (www.louisianaschools.com).

Key Accountability Indicators for K–12 Academics and Teacher Preparation—continued

the evidence supporting that intervention, and the partners who will assist them.[2]

Starting in 2019, LDOE will release annual public profiles of teacher preparation programs, which are intended to provide preparation programs with meaningful feedback, inform enrollment and hiring decisions, recognize programs for excellence, and identify and support those in need of improvement (LDOE, undated-q). Starting in 2023, the consequences for unsatisfactory performance include a corrective action period, an at-risk designation, a requirement for improvement plans, limited enrollment, or program closure (BESE, 2017).

_____

[2] More information on what schools must submit if they are labeled as requiring intervention can be found in *Louisiana's School System Planning Guide* (LDOE, 2017p).

At the time that these teacher preparation requirements were passed into policy, BESE also approved more than $7 million in transitional funding to support implementation of the new policies. The funding supports program administration costs, compensation for teacher training mentors, and compensation for residencies. This transitional funding will also support competitive applications from teacher preparation institutions for unique, high-cost needs (LDOE, 2017g).

BESE also established a quality rating system for teacher preparation programs, a state requirement under Title II of the federal Higher Education Act. In June 2017, BESE passed the policies that shape the quality rating system, after the preparation program design components became policy in late 2016. The rating system will be studied, refined, and phased in over a period of five years, with the first ongoing program approval decisions made in 2023 (LDOE, 2017g). A key component of these ratings systems is a program inspection, which is modeled on the inspectorate program that has been used by national education agencies across the UK since 1984 (LDOE, undated-s). Once every two years, a team of experts (four on average) will visit each teacher preparation program in the state and observe classes and clinical practice. The team will also conduct interviews with current candidates, program graduates, faculty, and staff. The BESE approved regulations for the teacher preparation rating system requiring that the rating system applies to all preparation providers equally, and that the system measures the quality of teacher preparation across three areas: the quality of preparation experiences, the extent to which the programs meet state workforce needs, and the impact teacher preparation programs have on student achievement growth and other measures of student learning.

Aligned Resources

Much of LDOE's work in both ECE and K–12 academics has focused on identifying, recommending, and even developing resources and tools intended to make it easier for districts and teachers to teach in ways that are aligned with state standards and assessments. As discussed in this section, those standards-aligned resources include curricula, formative assessments, and professional development. The state actions related to those resources include work to build educator awareness about what curricula and assessments are high-quality and aligned with Louisiana standards, as well as increase the supply of professional development aligned with those high-quality resources.

> **Action 3.** Signal to educators which instructional materials—including curricula and assessments—are high-quality, and which are not.

LDOE has created a coherent and aligned set of resources and tools intended to to make it easier for districts and teachers to teach in ways that are aligned with state standards and assessments. LDOE's theory of action focuses particularly on curricula as a mechanism for instructional improvement. In the words of one staff person involved with ELA and social studies curricula: "My biggest priorities have been around ensuring that we have the highest quality curriculum . . . and that districts and teachers are prepared to implement that curriculum." And, as mentioned earlier, one LDOE staff person focused on mathematics noted that if teachers are "really using" Eureka Math, then she can assume they are addressing the content of the standards.

Louisiana has aimed to ensure that districts and teachers have clear information about which curricula are high-quality. Prior to 2012, the state "adopted" a list of approved textbooks, and districts could only purchase from that list. One state official described that process:

> Committees would meet [every few years], publishers would bring in books. . . . They would review and decide to recommend [texts] that our state board approved. Districts could only purchase books off that list.

That old review process was put on hold while LDOE proposed a new process that it intended to be passed into law: LDOE would ask select Louisiana teachers to review materials, including online content, using a rigorous process that focused on alignment with standards. The process involved adapting rubrics originally developed by Student Achievement Partners and Achieve—a nonprofit education organization—to determine the alignment of materials with Common Core State Standards. LDOE proposed a rolling process whereby texts and other materials could be reviewed at any time and would be rated as Tier I (exemplifying quality), Tier II (approaching quality), and Tier III (does not represent quality).

By 2015—after extensive interactions among LDOE, textbook publishers, and districts to gather information about the best textbook review processes—the Louisiana legislature updated textbook adoption laws to match the review process LDOE proposed, and BESE updated policy regulations on the basis of that law. Districts were no longer required to purchase particular texts from a list. As one state official noted: "We actually got rid of that list deliberately, and we said purchase whatever you want. And at the same time, our job is to just tell you what's good and constantly keep that list as up to date as possible." Reviews of curricula and assessments then commenced.

In some cases, the state made the decision to develop curriculum materials that reflected its definition of quality and support open access to those materials. For example, the state developed ELA Guidebooks in collaboration with LearnZillion because it had not identified much in the way of Tier I ELA curricula. In social studies, it created scope and sequence documents that one state official noted were "hefty documents. . . . They're not just a yearlong plan, it goes down to the lesson level . . . basically a curriculum." LDOE is just beginning the new process of curriculum review for science.

Like Louisiana, many other states have processes in place that include review of curricula and official lists of "adopted" or "recommended" texts. However, unlike in other states, only a handful of textbooks have been recommended by Louisiana as Tier I materials, and many have been noted as Tier III (does not represent quality). In mathematics, for example, only four K–5 textbook products have been rated as Tier I by reviewers (Eureka Math K–5, The Math Learning Center—Bridges in Math, and Zearn Math), whereas 14 have been rated as Tier III. Furthermore, all the reviews are public, with clear information about the categories in which particular materials may have fallen short.[5]

All this is not to say that Louisiana state officials believe that getting good curricula into teachers' hands will solve everything. Interviewees were clear that giving teachers access to good curricula was just the first step in a process toward improvements in teaching and learning. Table 3.2 is a rubric available on the LDOE website that describes levels of curriculum implementation: that teachers have access to and use high-quality curricula, have some training to use it and modify it to support students, and—at the higher levels—can make thoughtful modifications that support students' diverse needs (LDOE, undated-d).

Louisiana is also one of the first states, to our knowledge, to review and rate formative, benchmark assessments for their alignment with state standards in both ECE and K–12 academics. As with

---

5   See LDOE (undated-k) for all reviews.

Table 3.2
Levels of Curriculum Implementation

Level	Description
Level 0	Low-quality curriculum in place.
Level 1	Teachers have access to high-quality curricula.
Level 2	Teachers have basic training that equips them with the knowledge and skill to use the curriculum "as written."
Level 3	Instructional staff facilitate and support the process of teachers modifying the curriculum to better meet students' needs.
Level 4	Teachers take full ownership for using information about performance to drive modifications to the curriculum and instruction.

SOURCE: LDOE, undated-d.

curricula, benchmark assessments are assigned a Tier I (exemplifying quality), Tier II (approaching quality), or Tier III (does not represent quality) rating. The categories of review for formative assessments are very similar to the main categories of LDOE's curriculum review. For example, for ELA, categories of reviews for both curriculum and formative assessments for grades 3–5 include Quality of Texts, Range of Texts, Text-Dependent Questions, Writing to Sources, and Speaking/Listening (LDOE, undated-k).

Louisiana has also created LEAP 360, which is an online assessment tool that supports formative assessment (LDOE, undated-l). LEAP 360 allows teachers to build online tests themselves, drawing on a bank of assessment items created by LDOE, and they can then receive performance reports on items aligned to state standards. There are currently more than 4,000 items in the bank, including items in ELA, math, social studies, and science.

Action 4. Increase the supply of high-quality, curriculum-specific professional development options, and provide clear information about those options.

LDOE has emphasized that high-quality professional development and assessments—from birth through 12th grade—should be aligned with Tier I curricula, and it provides an annual professional development course catalog of recommended professional development vendors. Vendors are included in the catalog only if their training is intended to help teachers use Tier I curricula, and vendors from across the United States have been included. Other criteria taken into account in vendor recommendations have included that the training enhances teachers' content knowledge and provides opportunities for teachers to practice their skills (LDOE, 2017h).

The *2017–2018 Vendor PD Course Catalog* (LDOE, 2017h) includes 26 vendors for ELA, mathematics, and social studies (as well as 11 early childhood PD vendors). For each professional development provider in the catalog, the following information is included: a description of the product, the timeframe for professional development, "Cost at-a-Glance," a contact, and which Tier I products are aligned with that professional development (e.g., Tier I benchmark assessments or curricula).

Incentives

Beyond mandates and resources, LDOE provides monetary incentives that encourage districts to follow mandates and adopt recommended resources. State actions related to incentives include discounted state contracts for resources the state has recommended as high-quality and—for teacher preparation—early funding for partnerships to test out and gather information about the intended teacher preparation model that would eventually be regulated through BESE requirements.

> **Action 5.** Provide funding incentives tied to use of high-quality curricula, professional development, and formative assessments.

Providing teacher access to good curricula is not a guarantee that teachers will use that curricula. LDOE curriculum reviews revealed that districts were not adopting Tier I curricula. As one state official put it, districts were "still eating at the one-star restaurants, maybe because they're cheaper or they're familiar with them." That staff member continued: "So we said basically, 'We'll give you a 10 percent coupon to that restaurant and we'll pay for your Uber,' and . . . if you tell people it's a five-star restaurant, and you give them a coupon, and you pay for their Uber, they show up."

The "coupon" comes in the form of state contracts that provide discounted rates and easy procurement of curriculum that it designated as Tier I. Specifically, LDOE negotiated pricing directly with Tier I vendors and completed the necessary paperwork with publishers to procure the materials. Districts that wished to purchase those materials just had to request to be included in the state contract and did not have to do any paperwork or negotiation to procure materials themselves. One state official noted that when the contracts went into effect, they "saw huge uptake, like, immediately."

In addition, Louisiana provided free professional development strongly aligned with Tier I curricula and—through LEAP 360—free formative assessments aligned with the items on the state's standardized tests. For example, the state has offered both teachers and leaders free regional professional development opportunities to learn more about Eureka Math and how to use it thoughtfully in the classroom. In addition, the state has put together remediation tools that include both formative assessments and interpretations of results that point to specific Eureka Math units and lessons that can be used to address students' difficulties. For grades 4–8 and Algebra, teachers can access a series of diagnostic assessments intended to be given before a teacher addresses a particular Eureka Math module or topic. The teacher is also given information about which standards are connected to particular diagnostic assessments and in-depth guidance on how to interpret students' responses to the diagnostic assessment in order to identify gaps in students' understanding of a particular standard. Lastly, teachers are provided with information about which Eureka Math lessons could address those gaps (LDOE, undated-e).

Some LDOE staff conceded that they have struggled to ensure that teachers are getting strong professional development aligned with Tier I curricula. One official told us,

> Professional development over the last three years has been our biggest, hardest nut to crack. . . . We don't have the capacity to

do that, and finding high-quality vendors who will offer training at a decent cost tailored to districts has been very difficult. And districts also tend to go with local people, they go with who they know.

Nonetheless, LDOE has been working closely with vendors to develop high-quality, content- and curriculum-specific professional development models that can be offered to districts across the state. Most recently, LDOE began a process to certify mentor teachers and content leaders who will then be charged with training teachers within their district. We describe that work in more detail in the communication and planning section below.

LDOE is now aiming toward a district funding model that ties all funding to a core set of academic criteria, and more specifically to whether districts' curricula, professional development, and assessments align with LDOE's definitions of quality. The state is currently developing those criteria, which will guide all funding decisions. While this process has been productive, one LDOE official noted that is has also been "complicated because we have to get the whole executive team to agree on that set of criteria about what makes a great school."

Action 6. Incentivize early adoption of the state's vision for high-quality teacher preparation through district-teacher preparation program partnership funding.

LDOE also incentivized teacher preparation providers and school systems to embrace the state's vision for high-quality teacher preparation, before policies were passed by BESE reflecting that vision. Specifically, before BESE passed regulations for yearlong residencies and a competency-based model, it awarded grants to district-teacher preparation provider partnerships, both to test out the feasibility of its definition of quality teacher preparation and incentivize providers to pursue that definition. Over time, LDOE became gradually more specific about what kinds of partnerships it would and would not fund. For the first cohort in 2014, LDOE set the guideline that the partnerships would provide teacher preparation candidates with opportunities to practice under a mentor teacher and would produce teachers in high-needs areas, including math, science, and special education. During this pilot phase, LDOE also brought participating programs together for professional development sessions, where they had opportunities to learn from one another's experiences and engage with national experts around these new preparation policy priorities. LDOE set more-specific guidelines for preparation partnerships as time went on. By the third year of the pilot phase, only partnerships that focused on residencies, produced teachers in high-needs areas, and included competency-based models could receive funding. By 2016, nearly 60 percent of Louisiana districts were involved in such partnerships. These expectations involved major changes on the part of providers, and LDOE made efforts to provide support to help with the transition. Currently, the state is in the process of scaling up the quality expectations, which are now codified into policy, across all districts in Louisiana, and it has provided additional transition funding to support those efforts.

Communication and Planning Processes

In this section, we provide more detail about how LDOE has used communication channels to identify champions and supporters for K–12 and teacher preparation activities, as well as gather information on obstacles and challenges to policy implementation.

> **Action 7.** Create communication structures to identify champions and gather information.

As discussed in Chapter One, LDOE interactions and communications with stakeholders are infused into its work at various points. In this section, we start by describing the communications and interactions that take place from the time LDOE has set goals for its work. These communications include LDOE efforts to gather information and identify champions for the work, as well as communications that support planning processes for various stakeholder groups.

The avenues through which LDOE communicates with stakeholders include calls or webinars, newsletters, and regional collaboratives. In addition, LDOE maintains regional networks that are also a touchpoint and source of professional development for districts. LDOE network leads spend most of their time interacting with school district leadership to communicate information about LDOE policies and processes and support districts in implementing those policies and processes.

While LDOE and its network leads communicate through different channels to district leaders, school counselors, principals, and teachers, LDOE strives to convey similar information about particular policies through each of these venues. In addition, state officials emphasized to us that representatives from multiple offices within LDOE weigh in on any communications or messages coming out of the department. For example, a state official noted to us that any guidebooks provided to stakeholders do not come from an individual team. Instead, LDOE divisions for academic content, academic policy, and teacher talent—among others—come together to agree on guidebook content. As one state official noted:

> I don't think anyone is reading [the guidebooks] cover to cover, [but] they're extremely helpful for us. . . . Those guidebooks force us to get clear on our shared message, clear on where we have gaps in our resources, clear on where we don't agree on the theory of change. And they take a good six to nine months to create one of those because of what we're trying to accomplish through the creation of that tool.

LDOE has relied on its communication structures early on in policymaking processes to gather information that can help shape policy priorities and goals. One LDOE state official noted that while the regional networks primarily focus on supporting districts, they are also an "ear to the ground." For example, network leaders might ask districts what aspects of standards teachers struggle with most or what materials they need, which can then feed into better supports for districts. Another state official described an "obsession" with why districts were not buying Tier I curricula. That state official spent considerable time talking to district leaders to understand obstacles to Tier I curricula adoption. She commented, "We just kept trying to find the barriers, find the barriers, find the barriers. . . . I wouldn't have even guessed on the front end half of the things we did would have mattered."

If districts found their board recalcitrant, they asked developers of Eureka Math from Louisiana State University to present at district board meetings. When districts expressed a need for a state contract to easily purchase materials, the state worked to provide them. When districts said that they needed a printer to print copies, LDOE implemented printing contracts. These are just some examples of how feedback gathered from stakeholders helped smooth and improve policy implementation.

In the area of teacher preparation, LDOE purposively started gathering information early to inform its work. In 2014, LDOE administered a survey to better understand the relationship between teacher preparation and school districts' needs. The survey included new teachers, faculty in teacher preparation programs, and administrators in schools and districts that hire from those programs. An LDOE official described the survey results as "a call to action for us, [that] kind of cemented our intent." One critical insight was the need for increased collaboration between teacher preparation providers and the school districts that hired graduates of the teacher preparation programs. Half of the preparation program faculty who responded to the survey said that there were not enough opportunities for student teaching, and almost 40 percent said that they lacked the information to identify appropriate mentor teachers. Only 39 percent of school and district leaders said that they regularly talked to preparation providers to create aligned preparation curriculum, and half of the teachers in the survey said that they were not fully prepared for the realities of the classroom when they entered the profession. Many district leaders (63 percent) also reported teacher shortages in specific areas, including science, mathematics, and special education, and nearly half of teacher preparation faculty said that they did not know enough about districts' staffing needs.[6] In response to these insights, LDOE reasoned that districts and preparation programs should collaborate to create better

---

[6] For more information on teacher shortages in Louisiana, as well as nationally, see Cross (2016).

practice teaching opportunities, pair student teachers with knowledge-able mentors, and improve the alignment between professional realities and teacher training. To facilitate these partnerships, LDOE launched the Believe and Prepare program in 2014 (LDOE, 2014a). LDOE will also release public profiles of teacher preparation programs starting in 2019, to both enhance public accountability for teacher prepara-tion programs and sustain a public dialogue around provider quality improvement.

Through its communication channels, LDOE has also worked to identify educators, districts, and other organizations who are willing to embrace its vision and then share it with others. These individuals and organizations have served to both champion the LDOE's work and provide clear models to emulate. LDOE has particularly focused on reaching out to educators. For example, starting in 2012, LDOE began recruiting "teacher leader advisers" who would be willing to help LDOE craft guidebooks and review curriculum materials, as well as deliver trainings and raise awareness regarding LDOE resources and tools. One state official focused on academics commented, "The first thing I did when I got here was attend a teacher leader adviser meeting. We've always had a small group of teachers to test things out and give us feedback. They're diverse and represent the state well. . . . We see them as an extension of our team." Teacher leader advisers are identi-fied through an application process that involves an instructional activ-ity and interview. The same state official commented that LDOE does a lot of training for teacher leader advisers but at the same time "want them to come with some pretty strong background on instruction." The number of teacher leader advisers is currently at 85. Each year, LDOE has tried to retain about half of the teacher leader advisers from the previous year while bringing in new teachers. They are provided with a stipend for their work.

In addition, the state has designated more than 5,000 teachers from across the state—about two teachers per school—as "teacher leaders," who receive both in-person and virtual trainings on state poli-cies, tools, and resources. For example, teacher leaders are invited to attend a Teacher Leader Summit each year, as well as regional collaboratives and summer institutes. Those teacher leaders are then expected to share what they have learned with others at their school.

The state is now working to identify and train additional teacher leaders within districts. In particular, it has used an application process to identify 200 "content leaders" who will sign on to receive in-depth training on content aligned with LDOE's vision for high quality instruction. These content leaders will then be certified to deliver training to others within their district. The state is also planning to use similar tools to train mentor teachers who support residents in the state's Believe and Prepare partnerships.

LDOE has also relied on districts to model quality implementation. For example, the state asked a small number of districts to pilot Eureka Math. One state official noted that this modeling was "really powerful" because those districts "saw good, pretty substantive gains in their math results in one year using Eureka Math." Similarly, LDOE piloted its ELA guidebooks with ten districts and summarized lessons learned from the pilot in a public report (LDOE, undated-f).

The Believe and Prepare partnerships between teacher preparation providers and school districts have also been models for others across the state, and the pilot partnerships, in particular, have benefited from being among the first to experiment with a new teacher preparation model. As one official noted:

> We wanted providers to be able to have the time and space to make changes with financial support as part of a community before we went to our board and said, now require these statewide. . . . I think that it created this really positive feedback loop. Residents were like, 'This is awesome. I love this. I'm so much more prepared.' Principals—number one—got better prepared teachers and—number two—had a guaranteed pipeline of teachers into their schools. There are just so many positive benefits that I think piloting it created a sense of possibility in the state.

In addition to identifying champions in the K–12 system, LDOE has also engaged deeply with vendors, both curriculum publishers and professional development vendors, to help them understand LDOE's definition of quality and create content aligned with that vision.

According to state officials with whom we spoke, textbook publishers had originally opposed legislation to update the curriculum review process. Then, at the suggestion of some legislators, LDOE formed a joint commission that included some textbook publishers and brought in district representatives to deliberate on the proposed curriculum review process. As one state official noted, that commission "ended up being really helpful. . . . It was helpful for the textbook publishers to have to sit in a commission where district person after district person said, 'Actually, we like the new process.'" State officials also noted that the commission deliberations helped them consider how to best shape the review process to support both districts and publishers. The commission produced a report (Task Force on Textbooks and Instructional Materials, undated) that helped support the curriculum review legislation, which was eventually passed in 2015. One state official noted that, with the new curriculum review process in place, publishers have reached out to LDOE for guidance to help them revise their materials to meet the state's curriculum review criteria.

Potential Implementation Challenges

As in other chapters of this report, we have provided only the viewpoints of LDOE on its policies and theory of action. We are missing crucial perspectives of key stakeholders charged with translating and implementing these policies. In subsequent reports, we will explore how stakeholders perceive and translate policies, and we will consider how policy implementation may be linked with changes in stakeholder behavior and student outcomes. In this final section, we outline key implementation challenges that we anticipate investigating in our subsequent reports focused on teacher preparation and K–12 academics.

Awareness and Understanding of the State's Vision for High-Quality Instruction

Leaders, teachers, and teacher preparation organizations cannot fully embrace LDOE's vision for high-quality instruction if they do not know about or fully comprehend that vision. We suspect that all the various communication structures within the state support awareness, but we know less about whether those structures also support deep understanding of LDOE's goals and vision. As pointed out in Chapter One, newer state standards and tests across the United States—as well as in Louisiana—are more rigorous than what has come before them, and any curricula, professional development, and teacher preparation competencies closely aligned with that definition of rigor are necessarily also ambitious and complex. Kaufman, Thompson, and Opfer (2016) provided a helpful starting point for us to examine more closely how well LDOE's ambitious goals are working their way into what teacher preparation providers, leaders, and teachers know and do.

Use of and High-Quality Support for Tier I Curricula and Formative Assessments

On a related note, LDOE partially defines *high-quality instruction* through the curricula and formative assessments that it has designated as Tier I, as well as through the professional development vendors it has identified as aligned with Tier I curricula and assessments. Yet no districts are required to use Tier I resources or recommended professional development (although they are heavily incentivized). As state officials pointed out to us, having fewer mandates may help persuade more districts to embrace LDOE's vision for education reform. Additionally, as we have already noted, many districts opted to use Eureka Math in particular, and LDOE has a sense that ELA guidebooks are being used by the vast majority of school districts in the states. At the same time, state officials believe that districts have been less quick to utilize professional development vendors who are supporting Tier I curricula and assessments. This crucial support is likely key to using Tier I resources thoughtfully and comprehensively. Most research recommends that teachers should receive curriculum-specific professional development to use curricula optimally (e.g., Correnti, 2007; Correnti and Rowan, 2007; Garet et al., 2001). Educators who do not receive curriculum-specific professional development may find it challenging to implement curricula in the spirit that it was intended. This may be an even greater issue with a curriculum such as Eureka Math, which may be more challenging than other texts (Kaufman et al., 2017).[7]

Timing Issues for Standards

LDOE has also faced timing issues that may affect high-quality implementation of social studies and science standards. For example, LDOE is putting in place a mandated science assessment that it intends for all students in 2018–2019. However, it has not yet identified full science curricula that will be aligned with science standards and assessments. As one official noted to us, "Districts are anxious about getting a quality curriculum in their hands and—unfortunately—I don't have the answer yet." Thus, some districts will likely be asking teachers to take on brand new science curricula in the same year that students' science scores will be taken into account in district and school report cards.

A state official noted that the same timing issues affected adoption of mathematics curricula aligned with state standards when the new standards were first put in place in 2010: "There was at least a few months' lag time between standards being adopted and curriculum being reviewed . . . and by that point, districts had already signed [textbook] contracts." Eventually, many districts opted to adopt Eureka Math, but it took time for those districts to come on board. While these timing issues may be somewhat inevitable, they may create anxiety among educators and schools who will be held accountable to help students master standards and may not feel they are prepared to do so.

Changes Within Teacher Preparation Institutions

Teacher preparation institutions face their own implementation challenges. While all teacher preparation institutions are moving to a new model focused on competencies and yearlong residencies, some institutions may just attempt to map old courses onto the new competencies while changing very little about the courses that they offer. Fur-

---

[7] A RAND study on EngageNY, which includes Eureka Math curricula, noted that teachers found the Eureka Math curriculum within EngageNY challenging, which they noted was both a positive feature of the curriculum and a negative feature when they were trying to support students below grade level. For more details, see Kaufman et al. (2017).

thermore, a yearlong residency requirement will change the model for how teacher candidates learn to be more focused on hands-on experience versus traditional coursework, which may not be an easy shift for faculty who are accustomed to traditional modes of instruction. In addition, institutions may make variable choices about what content is most important to include.

As the study progresses, we plan to talk with administrators and educators in district systems in multiple contexts to learn more about the challenges they face and how the LDOE has supported their work. We will also talk with teacher preparation institutions working in partnership with districts to learn more about what aspects of the partnerships have been productive and which aspects may have presented new challenges for both new teachers and those who support them.

CHAPTER FOUR
Graduation Pathways to College and Work

Louisiana students face a number of challenges to their success in the transition from high school to college and the workplace. For example, in the past decade, Louisiana has consistently ranked 47th in the nation in terms of the percentage of residents with two- and four-year college degrees; less than a quarter of Louisiana adults over age 25 completed bachelor degree requirements (U.S. Census Bureau, undated). Louisiana ranked 35th in the nation in four-year college completion rates; only 56 percent of Louisiana students who started in a four-year program finished within six years (Shapiro et al., 2017); this led some policymakers to conclude that students were not entering college adequately prepared. This puts the state and its workers in a precarious situation, as 65 percent of jobs nationally are anticipated to require postsecondary education and training by 2020 (Carnevale, Smith, and Strohl, 2013). Locally, the low rates of postsecondary completion have led to Louisiana industries facing a shortage of skilled workers to hire. Furthermore, while many of the projected new jobs in Louisiana are "middle-skill" (requiring high school and some additional training) (National Skills Coalition, 2015), not enough Louisiana students are obtaining needed credentials to get these jobs and meet the growing needs of employers in the state. Finally, students of diverse racial and socioeconomic demographics have uneven opportunities related to high school course offerings, attainment, college, and employment (The College Board, 2014). Yet, a significant amount of the available state and federal financial aid for both college and career and technical education (CTE) has gone unused (LDOE, 2017i).

To address these challenges, Louisiana has undertaken initiatives to improve the options that high school graduates have as they transition to college and the workplace. The goal is to both better prepare high school students as citizens and support the needs of the state economy (LDOE, 2017j). To do so, Louisiana has utilized mandates, aligned resources, incentives, and communication and planning strategies. Louisiana has relied particularly heavily on mandates that all students pursue a pathway to college or an industry-based certificate and complete necessary applications for postsecondary education while in high school. At the same time, the state has sought to hold schools accountable for results through indicators and public data. Louisiana has also provided resources and incentives, in the form of both structured provision of public school and externally provided courses and efforts to provide industry credentials to teachers.

As aligned with the intended theory of implementation we have already discussed, the state has piloted such initiatives as requiring all seniors to take the ACT and creating a leadership academy for CTE teachers, and the state has worked to better align high school course offerings with the preparation that students need for college and careers. Furthermore, to ensure that these initiatives are in line with expectations of postsecondary institutions and employers, the state has partnered and coordinated with these entities closely to plan and support implementation.

This chapter discusses Louisiana's goals for graduation pathways and then lays out how mandates have been particularly relied on, while resources, incentives, and communications have played lesser roles. The chapter concludes by describing remaining implementation challenges.

Key Goals and Actions

Louisiana has identified three goals to improve the graduation pathways of its students: improving career readiness to prepare students for "success in a Louisiana workplace," improving college readiness to promote "success in postsecondary education," and creating more options for postsecondary education finance to boost "economic opportunity."

More simply put, a Louisiana official that we interviewed described the graduation pathway vision as "providing meaningful, viable options to prepare our students for the 'what next'" so that "every kid comes out with some validated preparation for a funded next step"—whether college or the workforce. To meet these graduation pathways goals, Louisiana has undertaken seven key actions, listed in Table 4.1.

We discuss these actions and related initiatives in more detail below in the context of mandates, aligned resources, incentives, and communication and planning processes. Figure 4.1 summarizes the timeline for the major policies and activities that were part of this work.

Table 4.1
Graduation Pathway Actions in Louisiana

Action	Policy Lever
1. Require all high school students to pursue a pathway toward an industry-based certificate, postsecondary enrollment, or both.	Mandate
2. Implement graduation requirements that facilitate links with college and technical school admission and financial aid.	Mandate
3. Provide public data to hold Louisiana schools accountable on performance related to college and career readiness, valuing both tracks equally.	Mandate
4. Create course pathways that lead to high-quality industry credentials and preparation for certain college majors.	Resource alignment
5. Enable Louisiana teachers to have the credentials needed to implement the Jump Start pathways.	Resource alignment
6. Curate and fund access to quality external courses and credential opportunities.	Incentive
7. Draw on industry and higher education partners to select and create high school course pathways, based on regional workforce needs.	Communication and planning processes

Figure 4.1
Timeline for Major Policies and Activities for Graduation Pathways

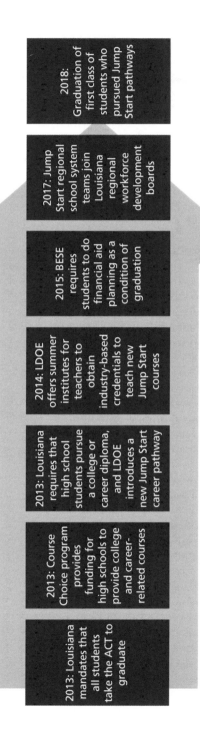

2013: Louisiana mandates that all students take the ACT to graduate

2013: Course Choice program provides funding for high schools to provide college and career-related courses

2013: Louisiana requires that high school students pursue a college or career diploma, and LDOE introduces a new Jump Start career pathway

2014: LDOE offers summer institutes for teachers to obtain industry-based credentials to teach new Jump Start courses

2015: BESE requires students to do financial aid planning as a condition of graduation

2017: Jump Start regional school system teams join Louisiana regional workforce development boards

2018: Graduation of first class of students who pursued Jump Start pathways

RAND RR2303-4.1

Mandates

Louisiana has used mandates to improve the quality of graduation pathways for students, including requiring students to choose a university pathway, an industry-based credential pathway, or both; requiring all students to take specific steps to attain college admission and financial aid; and providing public data on school performance related to college and career readiness. Definitions of quality sometimes relied on external sources, such as ACT scores or industry credentials.

Action 1. Require all high school students to pursue a pathway toward an industry-based certificate, postsecondary enrollment, or both.

Starting in 2014, Louisiana offered two high school diploma pathways—the Taylor Opportunity Program for Students (TOPS) University Pathway and the Jump Start TOPS Tech Pathway. Louisiana's Act 298 of 2009 requires that students choose one or both pathways to graduate. The new requirement encourages Louisiana high school students to plan proactively for either postsecondary education or technical training, or the workplace. In tenth grade, per LDOE guidance, high school students and their parents work with a guidance counselor to develop an individual graduation plan that reflects students' chosen pathways.

One state official described the goal as to "offer the appropriate pathways that align to the economic priorities of our state. But more importantly, we are preparing our students with the skills, the training, and the credentials they need to be viable candidates to enter the workforce pipeline." Another official noted that "pathways clearly spell out courses and work-based learning opportunities the kids can take to prepare for career and technical fields as well as for university admissions and state merit-based academic scholarships."

The TOPS University Pathway requires a set of courses for graduation that align with state requirements for both college admission and for a state university scholarship, so that students do not miss crucial steps to qualify for college and scholarships upon graduation. The Jump Start TOPS Tech Pathway requires a set of courses that lead to an industry-validated credential as a graduation requirement. Both of these pathways also set students on course to meet eligibility requirements for the TOPS Scholarship, which is a state scholarship program that pays tuition, and in some cases small stipends, to Louisiana students who are pursuing postsecondary education or training at a Louisiana college, university, or technical school (Louisiana Office

---

Alignment of Louisiana Graduation Requirements, the TOPS University Pathway, and TOPS Scholarships

The TOPS University Pathway requires students to take a core curriculum composed of college preparation coursework. The TOPS core curriculum includes the courses that colleges review for admissions, reflecting LDOE's desire for alignment across systems. This includes four years of English; a sequence of mathematics courses including Algebra, Geometry, Algebra II, and a fourth math course; four science courses; four social studies courses; at least two units of foreign language; at least one unit of art; and at least two units of physical education. Students select from menus of courses that are compatible with the TOPS University Pathway and TOPS Scholarships. These courses are weighted for the purpose of scholarship eligibility, with honors/AP on a five-point scale and standard courses on a four-point scale. College admissions requirements for Louisiana state schools (e.g., Louisiana State University, University of Louisiana–Lafayette, and University of New Orleans) list grade-point average expectations for some of these "core" curriculum/courses (Louisiana State University, 2017; University of Louisiana, 2017; University of New Orleans, 2017). LDOE also provides high school counselors with materials on how to support student decisions and planning related to pathways; it aims to ensure that students are getting a college preparation experience that will ready them to matriculate to four-year colleges.

of Student Financial Assistance, undated-a). See further details in the textbox.

Action 2. Implement graduation requirements that facilitate links with college and technical school admission and financial aid.

LDOE takes the view that "a high school diploma is no longer enough to earn graduates a living wage in today's economy. Some form of postsecondary education or training is essential" (LDOE, 2017j). Louisiana took two steps intended to increase college applications and attendance in the state, particularly among students with low college attendance rates, such as low socioeconomic groups and African Americans: All seniors must take the ACT in their junior year, and they receive financial aid planning as a graduation requirement.

In 2013, Louisiana mandated that all students—with the exception of students with significant cognitive disabilities—take the ACT as a requirement for graduation; the state funds and administers the ACT (LDOE, 2014b). State officials we interviewed believed that offering the ACT to all students would send a signal to those students who might not consider themselves "college material" that they could attend college if they scored well on the ACT, and the state committed to covering the costs for the ACT test to reinforce this view. Louisiana's decision to require the ACT echoes a national trend, as 25 other states and the District of Columbia fund and administer the ACT or SAT for all students (Adams, 2017; Gewertz, 2017). One recent study of 11 states found that offering the ACT or SAT to all students in a state boosted college-going rates, particularly among students who were less likely to take a college entrance exam before the policy and students in the poorest high schools. The requirement to take one of the college entrance exams was more effective in improving higher education attainment than traditional financial aid (Hyman, 2017). Students on the Jump Start TOPS Tech Pathway may replace the ACT requirement with the ACT-aligned WorkKeys exam, which is a career-readiness assessment measuring skills such as applied mathematics, business writing, teamwork, and more (LDOE, undated-h).

While it is still too early to fully assess the impact of the ACT requirement toward Louisiana's goals, statewide administration of the test has revealed several trends. All of Louisiana's graduating students took the ACT in 2017 as a diploma requirement, in comparison with the national state average of 60 percent (ACT, 2017b). At the same time, high ACT test-taking rates also highlighted some additional challenges. The average ACT score in Louisiana has remained at 19.5 since 2013, which is below the national average of 21.0 (ACT, 2017b). Only 8 percent of Louisiana students scored proficient in science and mathematics on the ACT in 2017, in comparison with a national average of 21 percent (ACT, 2017a). In the future, it would be useful for the state to analyze data about trends in college applications and attendance before and after statewide provision of the ACT, as well as trends in ACT scores over time.

LDOE officials also recognized that many Louisiana students were not taking advantage of the financial assistance resources available to them for postsecondary education and training, from both federal and state sources. One official summed it up: "What was happening was Louisiana was falling behind the curve. . . . It was below the national average . . . and just these hundreds of millions of dollars [of federal college financial aid] were being left on the table." In 2015, Louisiana had only a 48 percent Free Application for Federal Student Aid (FAFSA) completion rate, below the national average, with lower rates for poorer and underserved students (LDOE, 2017i). State officials hypothesized that showing all students how much financial aid could be available to them to attend college or CTE could increase the numbers of students continuing their education.

In 2015, LDOE worked with BESE to implement a policy to make financial aid planning a condition of graduating starting in 2018. In 2016, LDOE began rollout of the program, even though it would not become mandatory for another year. For seniors, LDOE officials and school counselors provided counseling to students on financial aid planning and filling out the FAFSA. In 2017, FAFSA completion in Louisiana (75 percent) topped the national average (61 percent) (LDOE, 2017i). Filling out FAFSA also gives students eligibility for other federal and state financial assistance, such as the TOPS Scholarship, the Federal Pell Grant Program, and Louisiana Education Loan Authority financial assistance. While FAFSA completion rates have increased, it is too early to tell how this has affected enrollment in postsecondary education.

Action 3. Provide public data to hold Louisiana schools accountable on performance related to college and career readiness, valuing both tracks equally.

Through their ESSA plan, Louisiana raised expectations for student achievement in several areas. The school and district ranking system supported these higher expectations by profiling schools

---

Key Accountability Indicators for Graduation Pathways

The many indicators of career and college readiness on high school report cards include ACT average scores and AP scores and the percentages of graduates earning 18 or above on the ACT or Silver and above on WorkKeys, graduating in four years, earning TOPS-aligned dual enrollment credits, and enrolling in college after graduating. In addition, as part of Louisiana's ESSA plan, the state developed a "quality of graduation" indicator. The quality of graduation indicator not only takes into account the numbers of students who graduate from high school, but it also considers students' credentials as they graduate. In particular, it gives equal weight to high-quality college preparation activities and to advanced industry-based certificates for non–college goers. The quality of graduation indicator puts some Jump Start credentials on par with AP 3 scores so that, as one LDOE official explained, they "built into our accountability that attaining Jump Start credentials is on par with the attainment of an AP score." The quality of graduation indicator was described by state officials as a "paradigm shift . . . around the perception of CTE, and we wanted them to value Jump Start the way that they value some of the offerings of the university pathway."

through school report cards that rank school quality using a letter grade and descriptive indicators. The state planned to raise the bar over time for the achievements that can earn a school an "A" grade (LDOE, 2015b; LDOE, undated-i). As discussed in the "Key Accountability Indicators for Graduation Pathways" textbox, report cards for schools contain a range of indicators relative to ratings for high schools, such as indicators related to college and career readiness. One official described how this is intended to incentivize schools and families to value technical education as much as college preparation, so that "now we have school administrators and district administrators recognizing that they can be acknowledged and rewarded in the accountability system in the same scale as that of their [college-bound] students."

Aligned Resources

Action 4. Create course pathways that lead to high-quality industry credentials and preparation for certain college majors.

In line with the mandate that all students choose and pursue coursework that leads to a college admission or career pathway with a culminating industry credential, Louisiana developed specific pathway options for students that schools could opt to include as part of their offerings. While most of these pathways were aimed at CTE, some also lead to preparation for specific college majors.

The most recent changes to Louisiana pathways have been the addition of new and more-rigorous CTE options for high schools through Jump Start, Louisiana's CTE initiative that aims to afford Louisiana students professional opportunities and positively impact the state's economy. As of 2017, LDOE offered 49 Jump Start pathways throughout the state. Not all pathways were available at all schools; offerings at each school vary according to regional needs, school decisions, and school capacity. Examples of the pathways included fields related to construction (e.g., electrician, plumber, carpenter), industry (e.g., mechanical drafter, crane operator, welder, manufacturing specialist), health care (e.g., nursing assistant, dental, health sciences

Louisiana's High School Welding Pathway

The welding pathway, one of Louisiana's Jump Start TOPS Tech Pathways, was frequently viewed as a model of the Jump Start program during our interviews with LDOE officials. It was developed based on the Louisiana Workforce Commission's projections for future high-wage, high-demand job availability, as well as in consultation with business leaders who intended to hire welding graduates. Employers in the state provided schools with machinery and materials for the courses, which saved districts considerable money. In return, employers "get a kid that's a certified welder that will go to work and understand what it means to be a welder." The LDOE website states that the entry-level salaries for the welding pathway range from $26,000 to $38,000 (LDOE, 2017n).

Students must obtain one of seven possible credentials to graduate, including American Welding Society credentials and National Center for Construction Education and Research certification, which will "provide students with immediate credibility among hiring executives in construction, manufacturing, maritime, and all related industry sectors, giving certified students an advantage in attaining entry-level employment" (LDOE, 2016e). Students in this pathway are required to take nine Jump Start course units in order to graduate (LDOE, undated-j). They take two fewer social studies and two fewer science courses than students in the TOPS University Pathway, and they are not required to take foreign language or art courses (LDOE, undated-j). This pathway does require the completion of a career readiness course.

patient care and management), and technology (e.g., digital media, information technology) (LDOE, 2017l). (See the textbox for a more in-depth discussion of the welding pathway, held up by many interviewees as an important model.) The "Early Childhood Education" pathway supports Louisiana's efforts to upgrade the skills of ECE providers. Pathways were chosen to be aligned with high-growth, high-wage job prospects in the state, as determined by state workforce development boards. The LDOE website provided information about the pathways for students, parents, and schools, laying out high school courses required, potential jobs related to the pathway, average starting salaries for these jobs, available internships and apprenticeships, and external certifications and credentials required for graduation (LDOE, 2017l).

Jump Start relied on external, industry-validated credentials for students to prepare them for employment, rather than on credentials provided by individual high schools; officials we interviewed noted that the intention was to signal to employers that students had externally validated credentials. Credentials were industry-specific and approved by the Louisiana Workforce Investment Council for high-wage jobs in high-growth career sectors. Students earn basic and advanced credentials that are recognized at the national, state, or local levels through dual enrollment coursework (e.g., ProStart as a food service certification, Emergency Medical Responder for the emergency medical tech pathway, National Center for Construction Education and Research for construction-related fields). Students may also earn complementary credentials, which are valued across industry sectors (e.g., Occupational Safety and Health Administration [OSHA] safety), as well as university dual enrollment credits through elective coursework (LDOE, 2017l).

In addition to the Jump Start pathways that lead to industry credentials by 12th grade, LDOE has worked to develop several K–16 pathways (i.e., pathways that are sequences of coursework from ninth grade through twelfth grade that aim to prepare students for and coordinate with coursework required in specific college majors). According to the officials we interviewed, the intention of K–16 pathways was to better prepare high school students for the college-level work that would be required of them in certain fields (e.g., engineering), and thereby reduce the number of college dropouts. As of 2017, LDOE had developed two K–16 pathways: pre-engineering and micro-enterprise (see the textbox for a discussion of the engineering pathway). LDOE is also developing additional K–16 pathways, including digital media design, biomedical, environmental management, and coastal restoration.

Louisiana's Pre-Engineering and Engineering K–16 Pathway

Launched in 2017 with eight schools in six districts, LDOE's Pre-Engineering and Engineering pathway was designed in partnership with Louisiana State University and the Cyber Innovation Center. LDOE advertises to high school students considering this pathway that the starting salary range for engineers who graduate with a bachelor's degree is $47,000 to $70,000 (LDOE, 2017m). Students in this pathway take eight courses in science, technology, engineering, and mathematics (STEM), two for each year (LSU, 2017b). But students do not have to elect the pathway until 11th grade, when more specialized courses start. These courses "expose students to principles of engineering, engineering design, computational thinking, data manipulation, robotics and economics, among other related topics" and allow students to earn college credit through dual enrollment courses at Louisiana State University (LSU, 2017b). High school graduates of this pathway receive a Louisiana State University Pre-Engineering Certificate of Completion as well as two complementary credentials from a selection of Safety and Computer Literacy credentials (LDOE, 2017m).

Action 5. Enable Louisiana teachers to have the credentials needed to implement the Jump Start Pathways.

LDOE recognized that the CTE teacher workforce would need additional skills to successfully implement the new Jump Start pathways. LDOE has taken several steps to develop the skills of its Jump Start teacher workforce. First, the state required that teachers of Jump Start courses must hold industry-credentials in the courses that they teach that deliver industry credentials. This meant that much of the existing teacher cohort would need to obtain new certifications in the technical classes that they taught. Beginning in 2014, LDOE, in collaboration with the South Louisiana Community College and the

Louisiana Community and Technical College System, offered intensive training each summer to teachers seeking credentials, at the "Jump Start Super Summer Institute." Training was offered for current teachers and for pre-service teachers. In 2018, according to LDOE data, Louisiana's 850 teachers who taught Jump Start courses had collectively obtained more than 1,000 credentials during the summer training institutes (in subjects such as construction crafts, business management and administration, health sciences, hospitality and tourism, information technology, and transportation, distribution, and logistics). A teacher could obtain more than one credential. The summer institutes were also meant to allow a wide range of teachers (in addition to teachers who were traditionally viewed as the CTE teachers) to obtain certifications. So for example, a social studies teacher could obtain a certification in Adobe. LDOE funded the summer institutes with some of the state's annual allocation of $20 million in federal Carl Perkins funds.

To further fill the teaching skills needs for Jump Start pathways, Louisiana also made additional use of the state's existing Career and Technical Trade and Industrial Education (CTTIE) certification, which enables people outside of the school system who are already industry-certified to obtain a teaching credential. Starting in 2014, LDOE with BESE approval took steps to streamline the CTTIE application process; in 2017, 391 people were teaching in a Louisiana public school with the CTTIE or related certification. One LDOE official described the purpose of this program as to "open up the talent pipeline to industry experts."

Finally, LDOE took steps to improve professional and leadership opportunities for CTE teachers. In particular, in 2018, it began piloting a new CTE leadership academy for teachers and school administrators. This was meant to be similar in concept to the teacher leader academies for other K–12 teachers. One LDOE official noted, "CTE is taking on a different connotation now. We think there needs to be a leadership pathway for these teachers, and it currently doesn't exist the same way it does for superintendents, principals, and teachers."

Incentives

In addition to mandates and resources, LDOE has also relied on incentives, such as making external courses available to schools and students to improve both college readiness and the quality of CTE programs on offer.

> **Action 6.** Curate and fund access to quality external courses and credential opportunities.

To support provision of high-quality pathways, Louisiana has offered students access to external courses that individual schools may not be able to offer through a program called "Course Choice"—also called "the supplemental course academy"—and has also linked with industry groups to provide pathways for students to earn external industry credentials as part of their high school degrees.

Louisiana developed the Course Choice program to provide additional per student funding at schools for online, community college, or other courses during high school. Course Choice started in 2013–2014 to provide funding to schools with students in grades 7–12. Initially, it did not include CTE courses, but in 2014–2015, BESE approved CTE providers to participate in the program.

When initially implemented, Course Choice was a controversial policy that met with teachers' union opposition. Union representatives believed that using funds to pay for courses taken outside the school violated the state constitution (Robelen, 2013). A Baton Rouge district court ruled the initial funding method (which diverted existing school resources toward external courses) unconstitutional as it removed public funds from the public schools to pay private enterprises. Following this ruling, Louisiana revised funding of the program, allocating additional budget for the new courses rather than diverting existing funds from the schools (Dreilinger, 2013).

In the 2016–2017 school year, the program had a budget of $7.5 million, covering over 40,000 student courses. The budget increased to $10 million in 2017–2018 (LDOE, 2017o) with 38 approved private course-providers in addition to Louisiana's public institutions. The most frequently used categories of courses were dual enrollment in colleges, ACT preparation, and CTE courses that students need for their Jump Start credentials. Courses were online, face-to-face, or a combination of both. Schools also received career development funds, for developing courses that help students work toward industry credentials. Funding could also be used for facilitating teacher professional development, student credential exams, and school capital investments. One LDOE official described course use:

> We give the flexibility to districts as to how they spend their funds to meet the unique needs of their students. So, it varies greatly. I can give you districts that use it all on dual-enrollment, I can give you districts that use it all for CTE, I can give you districts that use it all on ACT prep; it usually depends on their leadership.

Communication and Planning Processes

LDOE has developed a number of communication and planning processes to inform and facilitate changes in its graduation pathways for students, for stakeholders, and for regions. These planning processes engage industry and education partners in helping to shape pathway options to better ensure that students have the skills that they need to attend college or get jobs.

Action 7. Draw on industry and higher education partners to select and create high school course pathways, based on regional workforce needs.

Much like other current Louisiana reform strategies discussed in this report, the Jump Start program relied heavily on collaborative structures. Local Jump Start partnerships among schools, community colleges, and industry leaders were meant to create coherence between K–12 job preparation and industry demands. LDOE officials stressed the importance of "having all those stakeholders at the table to inform the development of those pathways." As of 2017, Jump Start regional teams composed of representatives of school systems have merged into the local workforce development boards, as an education subcommittee that helps to identify and validate credentials. Jump Start relied on these local partnership teams to develop or select CTE pathways, courses, credentials, and internships that connect high school students with workplace opportunities before and beyond graduation. Jump Start regional teams consisted of representatives from K–12 school systems, the local community and technical college system, regional economic development agencies, and business and industry. Jump Start regional teams were embedded in the eight development regions of the state. Each Louisiana high school offered different Jump Start pathways, so training offerings were context-specific and dependent on local partnerships, stakeholders, and interests.

Potential Implementation Challenges

While Louisiana has made significant progress in developing its career pathways strategies and initial rollout of key actions, several potential challenges to implementation remain. These include equity, state budget inconsistency, and regional variations in capacity.

Inequity of Access to College Preparation Coursework, Scholarships, and Particular Pathways

Our interviews and document analyses suggest significant impediments to students of low socioeconomic status and African American students to having equal opportunity for college attendance. Most TOPS Scholarship recipients in recent years have been white and middle to upper-middle class (Louisiana Board of Regents, 2015). Seventy-five percent of TOPS Scholarship recipients in both 2013 and 2014 were white, 41 percent had parental income over $100,000 in 2013–2014, and 58 percent had parental income over $70,000 (Louisiana Board of Regents, 2015). In 2011, 66 percent of Louisiana students were eligible for free or reduced price lunch, yet these students made up only 24 percent of graduates who took an AP exam and 13 percent of students who scored a 3 or higher on an AP exam (The College Board, 2014). Similarly, African American students made up 28 percent of AP exam-takers in the state in 2013 but amounted to 40 percent of those graduating from high school (The College Board, 2014). They also made up 17 percent of all TOPS Scholarship recipients in 2014 (Louisiana Board of Regents, 2015).

Students in rural or lower socioeconomic areas also have lacked equal opportunities. While Algebra II is typically required for entrance into a Louisiana college, not all schools in Louisiana offer Algebra II, according to state officials with whom we spoke. Therefore, students who attend these schools may be more likely to find their options limited merely because of where they lived. And as discussed in Chapter Three, there have been shortages of science and mathematics teachers statewide (Cross, 2016), particularly in rural or underserved areas, limiting options for students to pursue STEM careers. There are also differences in course offerings (for both college preparation and CTE) across schools.

State Budget Inconsistency

Louisiana has struggled to fully fund the TOPS Scholarship program for postsecondary education in recent years, despite its widespread popularity. TOPS Scholarships originally covered tuition fully for qualifying students attending public in-state institutions, and partially for students attending independent in-state colleges and universities (Crisp, 2016; Louisiana Office of Student Financial Assistance, undated-a). To qualify, students no longer have to be below an income cap, and they must reach GPA and ACT requirements, among others (Taylor Plan, undated). Colleges have recently raised tuition costs in response to budget cuts at the state level, thereby increasing the cost of the TOPS program (Deslatte, 2017). In February 2016, TOPS Scholarship payments were suspended due to a state budget crisis, and in the 2016–2017 school year, the state only covered 70 percent of eligible students' tuition costs (Deslatte, 2017; WAFB, 2016). In May 2016, the governor of Louisiana signed a bill into law that changed the TOPS Scholarship funding structure so that it was no longer tied to schools' tuition rates—instead, the amount of tuition paid per student at each school has been "locked in at the current rate" (Crisp, 2016). TOPS was once again fully funded in 2017. However, full funding meant that the scholarship now does not fully pay for students' tuition (O'Donoghue, 2017).

Regional Variations in Implementation Capacity

Variation in resources, leadership, and capacity among school districts has made implementation of these new initiatives uneven, according to LDOE officials. Multiple changes at once have been challenging for schools and districts, because the changes represent a "seismic shift" in policy and educational culture, as one LDOE official termed it. Multiple officials noted that some schools had come on board early, while others took longer. Other school and district leadership may not fully support changes by, for example, not cooperating on FAFSA requirements (in one example provided by state officials). Another described communication of changes as difficult with districts, schools, and parents, even with significant efforts to roll out information through workshops, announcements, and websites. One LDOE official described the variation: "The range is staggering; it's largely about leadership. It's partially about cultural traditions and money, but it's really just about leadership and awareness and interest on the part of the leadership." Some schools and districts may also face mismatches among the skills of their teachers and the skills that students need to meet workforce needs. Administrators may need to decide whether to retrain educators with new credentials, or hire new teachers.

Over the next year, as our study progresses, we plan to talk with high school administrators and educators in multiple contexts to learn more about how these efforts have been implemented, including the challenges they face and the factors that have supported their work. We will also talk with high school students to gather information about students' awareness of various supports and career and college pathways available to them.

CHAPTER FIVE

Conclusions and Next Steps

The previous three chapters described the key actions that Louisiana has taken to improve the quality of educational opportunities in early childhood education programs, K–12 academic instruction, teacher preparation, and pathways to graduation and beyond. The state has customized its approach in each of these areas by pulling on different policy levers to support student outcomes. However, at the same time, it has also approached reforms with an intended theory of implementation that particularly emphasizes communication and interactions with external partners and stakeholders. In this final chapter, we summarize some key themes that connect LDOE's work across different areas, which both reflect LDOE's intended theory of implementation and move beyond it. These themes may have implications for other states that are examining their policies and practices, and they provide some ideas that will guide our subsequent research to examine both policy implementation and outcomes across Louisiana in the coming year. We also briefly summarize some potential implementation challenges that we have identified throughout our report. Lastly, we share the next steps for our continuing work.

Cross-Cutting Themes Related to State Reforms

Clarity of Vision Around High-Quality Teaching and Learning
LDOE organizes its actions and theory of implementation around a particular vision of what constitutes high-quality teaching and learning. That vision is conveyed through LDOE's selection of measures and

87

indicators that are used for public reporting. CLASS, for instance, does not merely serve a measurement purpose, but is also intended to help define what high-quality care looks like for ECE providers through the rubric that lays out criteria for quality ratings. The use of local CLASS observers underscored this notion and enabled providers and their supervisors to use the information conveyed by the quality measurement system to benchmark practices and take steps to improve them.

What constitutes high-quality in K–12 is reflected in the Louisiana educator evaluation system as well. Yet, in our conversations with state officials, standards and assessments were emphasized more as the foundation for high-quality teaching and learning than the evaluation system. LDOE identified high-quality curricula and formative assessments that were closely aligned with K–12 standards and assessments and has worked to ensure knowledge of and access to high-quality curricula aligned with K–12 standards. The resources and tools that the state developed to inform decisions about curriculum, assessment, and professional development are extensive and have the potential to promote a coherent approach to instruction. In particular, the curriculum reviews, which are based on quality rubrics, along with the state's list of recommended curricula, help educators identify standards-aligned, high-quality resources to inform local decisions.

Interestingly, LDOE adopted a similar approach to K–12 for identifying high-quality ECE curricula in 2016, as well as incentivizing use of that high-quality curricula by lowering its cost. Yet, perhaps because the CLASS measures defined high-quality teaching and learning prior to the Initiative, both formative assessment and professional development appears to be aligned both with the CLASS and curricula that have been identified as quality.

Graduation pathways provide another example of the state's efforts to define and communicate quality through strategies such as Jump Start, which relies on external, industry-validated credentials. Moreover, by assigning equal weight in the school performance measurement system to success in college preparation and completion of vetted industry credentials, the state signals that both pathways are valued and can represent the culmination of a high-quality K–12 educational experience.

Close Adherence to Intended Theory of Implementation Apart from Federal Mandates

As we have noted, LDOE has articulated an intended theory of implementation that begins with data-gathering work to frame problems and test solutions, followed by efforts to identify points of coherence and alignment, and work to scale through partnerships. Ideally, full implementation of a mandate is put in place only after those prior steps have been taken. Then, the state develops and communicates planning processes for stakeholders to implement policies. We see more data-gathering and piloting taking place for those policy areas that are more under LDOE's control. In ECE, networks were piloted in 13 local communities in 2013, prior to scaling them across the state, and the performance profile rating system was only fully implemented in 2016–2017 after a practice year. In the area of teacher preparation, new preparation requirements were testing and piloting through Believe and Prepare partnerships prior to any legislation being passed. However, in the case of K–12, mandates for standards and assessments have not always been tested or piloted, likely because of timelines required by federal requirements in some cases. This could be an issue for upcoming science and social studies assessments, which may be required in the same year that schools are able to first try out standards-aligned curriculum and professional development.

At the same time, we have observed several aspects of the state's theory of implementation across reform areas. In particular, we highlight partnerships with educators and providers, as well as state emphasis on coherence and alignment as additional cross-cutting themes in our conclusion.

Close Involvement with Educators to Gather Feedback and Shared Ownership

As noted throughout this report, communication and planning strategies are a key element of the state's education reforms. LDOE has developed a variety of approaches to communication, both formal and informal, and many of these have particularly sought feedback from educators. By conveying the message that the state values educator input, state officials were able to communicate information while also

soliciting educator engagement and support. Networks and collaboratives have played a key role in these efforts. The early childhood community networks, for instance, provided a mechanism to gather feedback from stakeholders, including feedback from pilots of use of the
CLASS observation tool. These collaborations not only enable LDOE
to share information and get feedback, but they also promote learning among all partners to build their own capacity to implement state
policies.

In K–12, LDOE has long relied on a small group of teacher leader
advisers across the state to test out ideas, participate in initiatives, and
share their learning with others. Along with teacher leader advisers,
LDOE has also recruited a much larger group of teacher leaders from
nearly every school across Louisiana to attend and provide trainings, as
well as communicate with colleagues within and beyond their schools.
More recently, LDOE has been recruiting educators across the state
as both "content leaders" and "mentor teachers" who will be trained
to provide professional development both to teachers in the field and
teachers-in-training at teacher preparation institutions. LDOE's efforts
to identify and train strong teachers can seed expertise across schools
and districts, which could build both capacity and ownership of state-
led initiatives.

Partnerships with External Stakeholders to Provide Information and Support Scale

In every area of its reform efforts, LDOE works closely with external
partners to expand their capacity and reach. These partnerships serve
two roles. First, they help LDOE gather information and foster relationships that support buy-in. At the K–12 level, for example, LDOE
has engaged closely with publication vendors to develop and support
its curriculum policies. Similarly, LDOE has engaged closely with
teacher preparation providers and district leaders through the Believe
and Prepare program. Another concrete example of a communication
approach that has emphasized feedback is the ELA guidebooks, which
were piloted in a small number of districts, with the pilot data being
used to share information in a public report and to inform changes to
the documents.

For graduation pathways, engagement with industry to align educational programs with the needs of employers and provide training that they value similarly involved gathering feedback that local needs were being met. In all of these areas, clear, well-established structures for communication have solicited educator input to inform state policy and practice, and, according to interviewees, have helped promote buy-in and understanding of the state's priorities. These efforts also helped to expand the state's capacity to carry out communication and outreach activities, which in turn could help preserve funding and other resources for other activities.

Second, external partners and the private sector also play a key role in the provision of educational services in Louisiana, as they do in all states. LDOE has been strategic about creating structures and incentives to engage with private providers in recent years in a way that allows the state to maintain oversight and influence. For example, the state engaged with the private ECE providers and has developed mechanisms to regulate their work. Louisiana's rating system for private textbook companies for curriculum and for private teacher development training organizations has enabled the state to incentivize private-sector program developers and vendors to create products and programs that are aligned with the state's goals. As noted in the K–12 chapter, state officials' engagement with textbook publishers has helped them both pass legislation and policies supporting the curriculum review process and may be helping publishers to improve their textbooks. Similarly, the private sector helped select pathways, and Louisiana relies on private-sector industry credentials for some of them, while engaging in extensive communication with these private-sector organizations to ensure that these pathways and credentials meet the state's needs.

Coherence and Alignment Among Mandates, Incentives, and Resources

LDOE leaders identified several ways in which their work has been designed to create a coordinated set of aligned policies and practices that focus on student learning from the earliest ages through graduation and entry into postsecondary institutions. First, LDOE notes that the organization of its own department encourages coordination and integration of messages. Specifically, officials spoke of various divisions coming together to review communications and ensure consensus. In ECE, that coordination and integration was particularly supported by Act 3, which shifted governance and accountability for all programs in the state under a single umbrella. Second, LDOE has sought to align mandates with incentives, resources, and tools in all areas of its system. For example, in ECE, LDOE ties the curricula it has designated as high-quality with CLASS measures and the Teaching Strategies Gold formative assessment. In K–12, LDOE only recommends professional development that is explicitly aligned with high-quality curricula and assessments. In high schools, LDOE has strived to align college and career pathways with, respectively, course requirements for a college scholarship and industry-based credential. Lastly, the guidebooks that LDOE provides to all stakeholders are intended to provide a single, clear source of information about state mandates and associated incentives and resources, and officials from multiple divisions from within LDOE weigh in on those guidebooks.

Promotion of Equity Through Incentives and Resources

Concerns about equity have driven many of the state's actions. In ECE, Louisiana, like other states, lacked equitable access to high-quality opportunities. In some geographical regions, parent choice is extremely limited, so the publication of information about provider quality may not always enable parents to select high-quality options for their children. The state is working to reduce ECE inequities by increasing financial assistance to families through CCAP, but Louisiana still faces challenges to fully address the lack of high-quality choices in some geographic areas. In K–12, there are efforts to promote high-quality instruction for all students and to ensure that high-quality resources are available to all schools. One approach to resource provision involved the use of open curricula, open formative assessment systems, and free professional development that educators could take advantage of even if their schools are underresourced. LDOE is also working to address teacher shortages in high-need districts and schools. For graduation pathways, new course offerings and requirements are designed to improve opportunities for students in schools where they were previously lacking. The state has placed requirements on students to complete the FAFSA and the alignment of pathways with various scholarship opportunities. It will be important for the state to monitor whether these strategies enhance equity, work as intended, and provide the best value for the resources invested.

Quality Ratings for Both Processes and Outcomes, with an Increasing Emphasis on Outcomes as Students Get Older

The state has emphasized quality ratings as a means toward accountability, issuing mandates for public reporting of results, and creating incentives for educators and institutions to focus on key aspects of curriculum and student outcomes. Louisiana's approach to defining quality varies across the four areas we studied. In ECE, quality ratings focus on processes—namely the quality of instruction and classroom environment as measured by CLASS. Although state leaders referred to the system as being designed to improve outcomes, such as kindergarten readiness and social development, the CLASS measures themselves do not include outcomes assessment. The conceptualization of quality in K–12 involves both processes and outcomes, with a heavy focus on standards-aligned curricula along with reporting on student achievement and other student outcomes. For graduation pathways, quality also involves both processes and outcomes, but with a heavier emphasis on outcomes. Quality is defined partly in relation to specific pathways that schools offer, and industry-validated credentials play a role in providing criteria for coursework and assessing the quality of these pathways. The Course Choice policy, with its slate of authorized, pre-selected providers, also contributes to quality assurance. However, there are no clear quality criteria that are applied to the courses themselves. Quality is also defined in terms of student scores on the ACT and other outcome measures in school report cards. The examination of quality across the four areas indicates that the relative importance of outcomes versus processes increases with student age, consistent with a broader goal of ensuring that students have access to high-quality instructional experiences while developing the knowledge and skills needed for postsecondary success.

Some Key Implementation Challenges for Additional Study

Equity Issues Are Intertwined with the Capacity of Collaborative Networks, Early Childhood Centers, and Schools to Undertake State Reforms

LDOE's ambitious reforms require considerable changes to the education system in Louisiana, including but not limited to new Early Childhood Ancillary Certificate programs for ECE, high-quality implementation of new and more-rigorous curricula, enactment of new and untested models for teacher preparation, and inclusion of college and career-ready courses into high school curricula. All of these changes require high-capacity partners and school capacity to build educator knowledge. LDOE has been taking some necessary steps to build capacity by putting in place structures such as the ECE community networks and placing emphasis on the development of educator expertise. But resource needs are likely much greater in some areas of Louisiana than others, and, particularly, rural districts in corners of the state that are more difficult to reach and support. Louisiana has put in place a number of different accountability indicators to track the progress of ECE centers and schools. The extent to which the state can identify which centers and schools are falling behind will be key to the provision of additional support. Particular strategies to support more remote areas could also be helpful.

Educator Preparation Places a Strong Emphasis on Practical Experience, but the Effectiveness of This Approach Has Not Yet Been Determined

State leaders acknowledged the importance of practical, on-the-ground experience for candidates who are training to become educators. The Early Childhood Ancillary Certificate includes a requirement for practical experience, and K–12 teacher preparation emphasizes a residency requirement. State leaders mentioned the value of these practical experiences, which provide educator candidates with opportunities to develop and hone their skills through interactions with children in classrooms and schools, as ways to improve the quality of educator preparation.

At the same time, LDOE does not yet have the data needed to assess the extent to which these revised preparation approaches have been successful. This limitation is particularly salient for the Early Childhood Ancillary Certificate; the state lacks a mechanism to gather systematic information to gauge quality for programs that offer this certificate. By contrast, state leaders have engaged in extensive efforts to assess the quality of Louisiana's changes to K–12 teacher preparation: The state has a quality rating system for teacher preparation programs and has developed systematic processes to gather the data that inform these ratings. The diverse data sources that contribute to the program quality rating system for K–12 illustrate an approach to assessing program quality that can produce valuable formative feedback for program providers while helping prospective program participants evaluate their options. A similar approach might be viable for ECE. Although the state might lack the capacity to carry this out in a comprehensive way for early childhood, some elements of the K–12 efforts could be adopted at relatively low cost. For example, interviews with ECE teacher preparation program participants might be especially valuable as a way to gauge whether the practical components are providing the intended experiences, since it can be difficult to monitor the quality of these experiences in a direct way.

The State's Tradition of Local Control Likely Has Both Benefits and Drawbacks

Although Louisiana had adopted mandates to effect change, it has balanced this with the state's long tradition of ensuring that local education agencies have significant autonomy and influence over policies and practices related to education. This approach may have helped to promote widespread support for the state's efforts. It can also facilitate local experimentation with different approaches, which in turn can provide lessons to other educators or schools. The state's various networks provide one means to promote collaboration and communication around these local lessons.

At the same time, decentralization can lead to uneven implementation and has the potential to exacerbate inequities. In ECE, for example, the coordinated enrollment system is strongly influenced by local decisions, and we heard some concerns about individual program leaders' resistance to changing their enrollment procedures. While many districts have opted to adopt K–12 curricula that LDOE has recommended as Tier I curricula, officials also noted that districts still tend to choose professional development options that are not aligned with Tier I curricula or not curriculum-specific at all. The state lacks the capacity to offer curriculum-specific professional development in the same way that it has been able to provide access to and support to purchase Tier I curricula. LDOE strategies such as the multifaceted communication approaches and the provision of curriculum resources and technical assistance are likely to help mitigate some of the potential drawbacks of local control, but continued monitoring and provision of guidance and resources where needed will be crucial for promoting statewide adoption of high-quality programming and practices.

Next Steps

This research has pointed to policy reforms over the past several years that could lead to better outcomes for Louisiana students. However, the state strategies and actions discussed in this report convey only one piece of the puzzle constituting Louisiana's education reforms. All the information conveyed in this report has been gathered only from state officials and documents that describe LDOE's approach in various areas. We have not yet gathered information from stakeholders across the system to examine both policy implementation and outcomes.

As part of our ongoing work in Louisiana, we will be examining the following three questions:

1. How are the state's actions being perceived and translated on the ground by key stakeholders who serve students?
2. What evidence connects state actions with change in what stakeholders do?

3.   What evidence connects state actions with changes in child and student outcomes?

We will be conducting case studies and collecting additional data to answer these questions. For the first question, in particular, we will consider whether we see any evidence reflecting the potential implementation challenges highlighted in this report. Perceptions of stakeholders may shed light on that, as well as the extent to which the themes in this report are playing out on the ground with leaders, teachers, and students. For example: How do stakeholders define quality teaching and learning, and how do those definitions align with how the state defines quality? How much buy-in do we observe in regard to state policies and messages, and what are the main vehicles that appear to promote buy-in? Can stakeholders clearly identify points of alignment and coherence in the education system? We will closely examine those and other questions in our forthcoming work.

In addition, while Louisiana has seen some small improvements to student achievement that we have discussed briefly in this report, some improvements may not become apparent for a few more years. As part of our ongoing work in Louisiana, we will be examining outcomes that could be connected with the policy reforms we have highlighted in this report. Such outcomes include those related to school practices, like curriculum adoption and provision of professional development, as well as a range of student outcomes. We expect to release an additional report in 2019 that summarizes findings from our additional research.

Final Thoughts

This report has provided a detailed description of Louisiana's approach to improving educational experiences and student outcomes in early childhood education, K–12 academics and K–12 teacher preparation, and graduation pathways. This analysis should be of interest to other states, for a few reasons. First, Louisiana has seen growth in several important student outcomes in recent years, and teachers in the state report higher levels of standards implementation than teachers in other states, on average. Despite these areas of success, however, Louisiana continues to face significant challenges, particularly related to equity of educational opportunities and outcomes. Thus, a second factor that makes this analysis potentially useful to other states is that Louisiana is grappling with many of the same challenges that are confronting states across the United States, and its experiences offer an example of how one state has addressed them.

Yet, as we noted in Chapter One, it is too early to know the extent to which any of the strategies described in this report will achieve their intended goals. We are not advocating for any of the specific strategies we describe, and this report is not intended to outline a suggested approach to state policy in any areas we have examined. Each state must develop policies and practices that align with its unique goals and context, and it would be unwise for one state to adopt another's approach without keeping these differences in mind. This report provides examples of the various actions and policy levers other states could use to support education improvements in a variety of areas. However, which actions and levers states choose to leverage could depend on a variety of factors, including areas where the state might have more or less authority over policy and how much reform has already taken place. Our intention with this report is to provide other states with examples of possibilities based on Louisiana's work. States can then reflect on what those possibilities might imply for their own policymaking, while also considering the mechanisms through which Louisiana might be achieving its ambitious goals.

References

Achieve, *Strong Standards: A Review of Changes to State Standards Since the Common Core*, Washington, D.C., 2017. As of November 15, 2017: https://www.achieve.org/files/StrongStandards.pdf

ACT, *The ACT Profile Report—State: Graduating Class 2017, Public High School Students, Louisiana*, 2017a.

———, *Average ACT Scores by State Graduating Class*, 2017b. As of November 6, 2017: http://www.act.org/content/dam/act/unsecured/documents/cccr2017/ACT_2017-Average_Scores_by_State.pdf

Adams, Caralee J., "In Race for Test-Takers, ACT Outscores SAT—for Now," *Education Week*, Vol. 36, No. 32, 2017, pp. 22–23.

BESE—*See* Louisiana Board of Elementary and Secondary Education.

Bishaw, Alemayehu, and Craig Benson, *Poverty: 2015 and 2016*, Washington, D.C.: U.S. Census Bureau, 2017. As of November 14, 2017: https://www.census.gov/content/dam/Census/library/publications/2017/acs/acsbr16-01.pdf

Bjorklund-Young, Alanna and David Steiner, *The 2017 NAEP Results: Why a Full, Public Data Release Matters*, Johns Hopkins School of Education, Institute for Education Policy, 2018. As of April 13, 2018: https://www.the74million.org/wp-content/uploads/2018/04/NAEP-Review-Memo-Johns-Hopkins.pdf

Carnevale, Anthony P., Nicole Smith, and Jeff Strohl, *Recovery: Job Growth and Education Requirements Through 2020*, Georgetown University, 2013. As of November 14, 2017: https://cew.georgetown.edu/wp-content/uploads/2014/11/Recovery2020.FR_.Web_.pdf

Chiefs for Change, *Hiding in Plain Sight: Leveraging Curriculum to Improve Student Learning*, 2017. As of November 14, 2017: http://chiefsforchange.org/policy-paper/4830/

Coburn, Cynthia E., Heather C. Hill, and James P. Spillane, "Alignment and Accountability in Policy Design and Implementation: The Common Core State Standards and Implementation Research," *Educational Researcher*, Vol. 45, No. 4, 2016, pp. 243–251.

The College Board, *The 10th Annual AP Report to the Nation: Louisiana Supplement*, 2014. As of November 13, 2017: http://media.collegeboard.com/digitalServices/pdf/ap/rtn/10th-annual/10th-annual-ap-report-state-supplement-louisiana.pdf

Correnti, Richard, "An Empirical Investigation of Professional Development Effects on Literacy Instruction Using Daily Logs," *Educational Evaluation and Policy Analysis*, Vol. 29, No. 4, 2007, pp. 262–295.

Correnti, Richard, and Brian Rowan, "Opening Up the Black Box: Literacy Instruction in Schools Participating in Three Comprehensive School Reform Programs," *American Educational Research Journal*, Vol. 44, No. 2, 2007, pp. 298–339.

Crisp, Elizabeth, "Major Change to TOPS Scholarships Signed Into Law; Here's How It Affects Louisiana Students," *The Advocate*, May 10, 2016. As of November 6, 2017: http://www.theadvocate.com/baton_rouge/news/politics/legislature/article_ccdc91f1-71a9-5c0c-b861-9fc97a761f66.html

Cronin, John, Michael Dahlin, Deborah Adkins, and G. Gage Kingsbury. *The Proficiency Illusion*, Washington, D.C.: Thomas B. Fordham Institute, 2007.

Cross, Freddie, *Teacher Shortage Areas Nationwide Listing 1990–1991 Through 2016–2017*, U.S. Department of Education: Office of Postsecondary Education, 2016. As of November 14, 2017: https://www2.ed.gov/about/offices/list/ope/pol/tsa.pdf

DePascale, Charles A. *Review of Comparability Claims for the 2017 LEAP Assessments: A Memorandum to the Louisiana Department of Education*, Dover, N.H.: Center for Assessment, 2017.

Deslatte, Melinda, "TOPS Again a Target in Louisiana Session, Budget Negotiation," *Associated Press*, April 6, 2017. As of November 6, 2017: https://www.usnews.com/news/best-states/louisiana/articles/2017-04-06/tops-again-a-target-in-louisiana-session-budget-negotiation

Dreilinger, Danielle, "State's Course Choice Program to Give Students Option to Take Outside Classes, but Financing and Implementation Still Face Hurdles," *NOLA.com/The Times-Picayune*, January 11, 2013. As of November 14, 2017: http://www.nola.com/education/index.ssf/2013/01/states_course_choice_program_m.html

Education Week Research Center, *School Finance*, 2016. As of November 14, 2017: https://secure.edweek.org/media/school-finance-education-week-quality-counts-2016.pdf

Fuhrman, Susan, William Clune, and Richard Elmore, "Research on Education Reform: Lessons on the Implementation of Policy," in Allan R. Odden, ed., *Education Policy Implementation*, Albany, N.Y.: State University of New York Press, 1991.

Garet, Michael S., Andrew C. Porter, Laura Desimone, Beatrice F. Birman, and Kwang Suk Yoon, "What Makes Professional Development Effective? Results from a National Sample of Teachers," *American Educational Research Journal*, Vol. 38, No. 4, Winter 2001, pp. 915–945.

Gewertz, Catherine, "Which States Require Students to Take the SAT or ACT? An Interactive Breakdown of States' 2016–17 Testing Plans," *Education Week*, Vol. 36, No. 21, February 15, 2017.

Heath, Chip, and Dan Heath, *Made to Stick: Why Some Ideas Survive and Others Die*, New York: Random House, 2007.

Honig, Meredith I., "Complexity and Policy Implementation: Challenges and Opportunities for the Field," in Meredith I. Honig, ed., *New Directions in Education Policy Implementation: Confronting Complexity*, Albany, N.Y.: State University of New York Press, 2006, pp. 1–24.

Hyman, Joshua, "ACT for All: The Effect of Mandatory College Entrance Exams on Postsecondary Attainment and Choice," *Education Finance and Policy*, June 27, 2017.

Kaufman, Julia H., John S. Davis II, Elaine Lin Wang, Lindsey E. Thompson, Joseph D. Pane, Katherine Pfrommer, and Mark Harris, *Use of Open Educational Resources in an Era of Common Standards: A Case Study on the Use of EngageNY*, Santa Monica, Calif.: RAND Corporation, RR-1773-BMGF, 2017. As of November 14, 2017:
https://www.rand.org/pubs/research_reports/RR1773.html

Kaufman, Julia H., Lindsey E. Thompson, and V. Darleen Opfer, *Creating a Coherent System to Support Instruction Aligned with State Standards: Promising Practices of the Louisiana Department of Education*, Santa Monica, Calif.: RAND Corporation, RR-1613-HCT, 2016. As of November 09, 2017:
https://www.rand.org/pubs/research_reports/RR1613.html

Korn, Shira, Martin Gamboa, and Morgan Polikoff, *Just How Common Are the Standards in Common Core States?* Philadelphia, Pa.: Pennsylvania University, The Center on Standards, Alignment, Instruction, and Learning, 2016. As of November 15, 2017:
http://c-sail.org/resources/blog/
just-how-common-are-standards-common-core-states

Ladd, Helen, "No Child Left Behind: A Deeply Flawed Federal Policy," *Journal of Policy Analysis and Management*, Vol. 36, No. 2, January 30, 2017, pp. 461–469.

La Paro, Karen M., Amy C. Williamson, and Bridget Hatfield, "Assessing Quality in Toddler Classrooms Using the CLASS-Toddler and the ITERS-R," *Early Education and Development*, Vol. 25, No. 6, 2014, pp. 875–893.

Layton, Lyndsey, "Louisiana Gov. Bobby Jindal Sues Obama over Common Core State Standards," *Washington Post*, August 27, 2014.

LDOE—*See* Louisiana Department of Education.

Louisiana Board of Elementary and Secondary Education, "BESE Rulemaking Docket," webpage, 2017. As of November 14, 2017:
http://bese.louisiana.gov/documents-resources/rulemaking-docket

Louisiana Board of Regents, *TOPS Report: Analysis of the TOPS Program from 2005–2014*, Baton Rouge, La., 2015. As of November 14, 2017:
http://www.regents.la.gov/assets/BOROctober/TOPS2015.pdf

Louisiana Department of Education, ed., *Louisiana's Kindergarten Readiness Definition*, Baton Rouge, La., undated-a. As of November 14, 2017:
http://www.louisianabelieves.com/docs/default-source/early-childhood/brochure---kindergarten-readiness-definition-(english).pdf?sfvrsn=5

———, *Believe and Prepare: Early Childhood Cohort 3 Request for Applications*, Baton Rouge, La., undated-b. As of November 14, 2017:
https://www.louisianabelieves.com/docs/default-source/early-childhood/believe-and-prepare---early-childhood---cohort-3---request-for-applications.pdf?sfvrsn=4

———, *Science Standards: Shifts in Science*, Baton Rouge, La., undated-c. As of November 14, 2017:
https://www.louisianabelieves.com/docs/default-source/teacher-toolbox-resources/science-standards---shifts-in-science.pdf?sfvrsn=3

———, "Curriculum Implementation Scale," Baton Rouge, La., undated-d. As of November 14, 2017:
https://www.louisianabelieves.com/docs/default-source/Superintendents-Collaboration/curriculum-implementation-scale.pdf?sfvrsn=2

———, "K–12 Math Planning Resources," webpage, undated-e. As of November 14, 2017:
http://www.louisianabelieves.com/resources/library/k-12-math-year-long-planning

———, *ELA Guidebooks 2.0: Pilot Feedback Report*, Baton Rouge, La., undated-f. As of November 14, 2017:
http://www.louisianabelieves.com/docs/default-source/teacher-toolbox-resources/ela-guidebooks-2-0-feedback-report.pdf?sfvrsn=2

———, "Financial Aid for Students," webpage, undated-g. As of November 14, 2017:
http://www.louisianabelieves.com/courses/financialaid

————, *High School Assessments Fact Sheet*, Baton Rouge, La., undated-h. As of November 6, 2017:
http://www.louisianabelieves.com/docs/default-source/assessment/high-school-assessments-fact-sheet.pdf?sfvrsn=4

————, "School and Early Childhood Program Performance," webpage, undated-i. As of November 6, 2017:
http://www.louisianabelieves.com/assessment/school-and-center-performance

————, "Graduation Requirements," webpage, undated-j. As of November 14, 2017:
https://www.louisianabelieves.com/courses/graduation-requirements

————, "Curricular Resources Annotated Reviews," webpage, undated-k. As of December 18, 2017:
http://www.louisianabelieves.com/academics/ONLINE-INSTRUCTIONAL-MATERIALS-REVIEWS/curricular-resources-annotated-reviews

————, "LEAP 360," webpage, undated-l. As of December 18, 2017:
https://www.louisianabelieves.com/measuringresults/leap-360

————, *Third Party Guide*, Lafayette, La., undated-m. As of January 28, 2017:
http://www.louisianabelieves.com/docs/default-source/early-childhood/third-party-guide.pdf?sfvrsn=2

————, "Louisiana Schools," webpage, undated-n. As of February 1, 2018:
http://www.louisianaschools.com/

————, "Preschool Expansion Grant Overview," webpage, undated-o. As of April 18, 2018:
https://www.louisianabelieves.com/docs/default-source/early-childhood/preschool-expansion-grant-overview.pdf?sfvrsn=2

————, "Program Description," webpage, undated-p. As of April 18, 2018:
https://www.prekla.org/parents/program.html

————, "Teacher Preparation Quality Rating System," undated-q. As of April 18, 2018:
https://www.louisianabelieves.com/docs/default-source/key-initiatives/louisianas-key-initiatives_teacher-preparation-quality-rating-system.pdf?sfvrsn=5

————, "Child Care Assistance Application Process," undated-r. As of May 14, 2018:
https://www.louisianabelieves.com/docs/default-source/child-care-providers/ccap-application-process-flowchart.pdf?sfvrsn=2

————, "Teacher Preparation On-Site Review Brief," undated-s. As of April 18, 2018:
https://www.louisianabelieves.com/docs/default-source/teaching/teacher-preparation-onsite-review-brief_january-2017.pdf?sfvrsn=6

———, *Fall 2013 Reading Report: School, District, and State Results for Kindergarten Through Third Grade*, Baton Rouge, La., 2013a. As of January 28, 2017:
https://www.louisianabelieves.com/docs/default-source/test-results/fall-2013-dibels-reading-report.pdf?sfvrsn=2

———, *Louisiana's Birth to Five Early Learning and Development Standards (ELDS)*, Baton Rouge, La., 2013b. As of November 13, 2017:
http://www.louisianabelieves.com/docs/default-source/academic-standards/early-childhood---birth-to-five-standards.pdf?sfvrsn=6

———, *Partners in Preparation: A Survey of Educators & Education Preparation Programs*, Baton Rouge, La., 2014a. As of November 14, 2017:
https://www.louisianabelieves.com/docs/default-source/links-for-newsletters/partners-in-preparation-survey-report.pdf?sfvrsn=6

———, "Report Shows Record Number of Louisiana Students Achieving College-Level ACT Scores," Baton Rouge, La., 2014b. As of November 6, 2017:
https://www.louisianabelieves.com/newsroom/news-releases/2014/08/20/report-shows-record-number-of-louisiana-students-achieving-college-level-act-scores

———, "BESE Plan Makes Child Care Affordable for Low-Income Louisiana Families," Baton Rouge, La., 2015a. As of November 13, 2017:
http://www.louisianabelieves.com/newsroom/news-releases/2015/08/12/bese-plan-makes-child-care-affordable-for-low-income-louisiana-families

———, *Louisiana's Plan for Ensuring Equitable Access to Excellent Teachers for All Students*, Baton Rouge, La., 2015b. As of November 6, 2017:
http://www.louisianabelieves.com/docs/default-source/equity/louisiana-state-equity-plan.pdf?sfvrsn=2

———, *Child Care Curriculum Initiative Guidance*, Baton Rouge, La., 2016a. As of November 14, 2017:
https://www.louisianabelieves.com/docs/default-source/early-childhood/child-care-curriculum-initiative-packet.pdf?sfvrsn=6

———, *Fall 2016 Reading Report: School, District, and State Results for Kindergarten Through Grade Three*, Baton Rouge, La., 2016b. As of November 13, 2017:
https://www.louisianabelieves.com/docs/default-source/test-results/fall-2016-dibels-reading-report.pdf?sfvrsn=4

———, *Guide to Success for Early Childhood Community Network Lead Agencies*, Baton Rouge, La., 2016c. As of November 14, 2017:
http://www.louisianabelieves.com/docs/default-source/early-childhood/2016-early-childhood-louisiana-guidebook.pdf?sfvrsn=16

————, *K–12 Student Standards for English Language Arts*, Baton Rouge, La., 2016d. As of November 14, 2017:
http://www.louisianabelieves.com/docs/default-source/teacher-toolbox-resources/K-12-ela-standards.pdf?sfvrsn=36

————, *National Center for Construction Education and Research (NCCER): Welding Level Combined*, Baton Rouge, La., 2016e. As of November 14, 2017:
http://www.louisianabelieves.com/docs/default-source/jumpstart/nccer-welding-combined.pdf?sfvrsn=11

————, *Louisiana's Early Childhood Care and Education Network: Update for the Field*, Baton Rouge, La., 2017a. As of November 14, 2017:
https://www.louisianabelieves.com/docs/default-source/early-childhood/2017-2018-policy-and-practice-updates-for-the-field-presentation.pdf?sfvrsn=8

————, *Louisiana's Pre–K Through Third Grade Guidebook for Sites and System Leaders*, Baton Rouge, La., 2017b. As of November 14, 2017:
https://www.louisianabelieves.com/docs/default-source/early-childhood/louisianas-pre-k-through-third-grade-guidebook-for-site-and-system-leaders.pdf

————, "Transforming Early Childhood in Louisiana: 2012–2017," unpublished PowerPoint, 2017c.

————, *Accountability Policy Update*, Baton Rouge, La., 2017d. As of November 14, 2017:
http://www.louisianabelieves.com/docs/default-source/louisiana-believes/essa-accountability-plan-summary.pdf?sfvrsn=12

————, *2016–2017 School and Center Performance*, Baton Rouge, La., 2017e. As of November 14, 2017:
https://www.louisianabelieves.com/docs/default-source/data-management/2017-school-and-early-childhood-performance-score-media-briefing.pdf?sfvrsn=4

————, *K–12 Louisiana Student Standards for Mathematics*, Baton Rouge, La., 2017f. As of November 14, 2017:
http://www.louisianabelieves.com/docs/default-source/teacher-toolbox-resources/louisiana-student-standards-for-K–12-math.pdf?sfvrsn=52

————, *Updated Teacher Preparation Transition Guide*, Baton Rouge, La., 2017g. As of November 14, 2017:
http://www.louisianabelieves.com/docs/default-source/teaching/teacher-preparation-transition-guide.pdf?sfvrsn=6

————, *2017–2018 Vendor PD Course Catalog*, Baton Rouge, La., 2017h. As of November 14, 2017:
http://www.louisianabelieves.com/docs/default-source/teacher-toolbox-resources/vendor-pd---course-catalog.pdf?sfvrsn=16

———, *The State of Financial Aid in Louisiana: A Report of the Louisiana Financial Aid Working Group*, Baton Rouge, La., 2017i. As of November 14, 2017: https://www.louisianabelieves.com/docs/default-source/course-choice/the-state-of-financial-aid-in-louisiana.pdf?sfvrsn=2

———, *Louisiana's High School Student Planning Guidebook: A Path to Prosperity for Every Student*, Baton Rouge, La., 2017j. As of November 6, 2017: http://www.louisianabelieves.com/docs/default-source/course-choice/high-school-planning-guidebook-(web).pdf?sfvrsn=26

———, "ACT' Scores Increase for Fourth Straight Year in Louisiana Public Schools," Baton Rouge, La., 2017k. As of November 6, 2017: https://www.louisianabelieves.com/newsroom/news-releases/2017/08/09/act-scores-increase-for-fourth-straight-year-in-louisiana-public-schools

———, "Jump Start Graduation Pathways Master Spreadsheet," webpage, 2017l. As of November 6, 2017: https://www.louisianabelieves.com/resources/library/jump-start-graduation-pathways

———, *Proposed 2017–2018 Graduation Pathway: Pre-Engineering*, Baton Rouge, La., 2017m. As of November 14, 2017: http://www.louisianabelieves.com/docs/default-source/js-graduation-pathways/2017-2018-pre-engineering-pathway-pdf.pdf?sfvrsn=3

———, *Approved 2017–2018 Graduation Pathway: Welder*, Baton Rouge, La., 2017n. As of November 14, 2017: http://www.louisianabelieves.com/docs/default-source/js-graduation-pathways/2017-2018-welder-pathway-pdf.pdf?sfvrsn=3

———, *What Is Supplemental Course Allocation/Course Choice (SCA)?*, Baton Rouge, La., 2017o. As of November 6, 2017: https://www.louisianabelieves.com/docs/default-source/key-initiatives/louisianas-key-initiatives_course-choice.pdf?sfvrsn=

———, *Louisiana's School System Planning Guide, 2017–18*, Baton Rouge, La., 2017p. As of January 31, 2018: http://www.louisianabelieves.com/docs/default-source/district-support/louisianas-school-system-planning-guide.pdf

———, *Compass Implementation 2017–18,* Baton Rouge, La., 2017q. As of May 14, 2018: https://www.louisianabelieves.com/docs/default-source/key-compass-resources/hr-directors-compass-2017-2018-august.pdf?sfvrsn=4

———, "Frequently Asked Questions: Child Care Assistance Program (CCAP) Application Process for Households," June 1, 2017r. As of May 14, 2018: https://www.louisianabelieves.com/docs/default-source/child-care-providers/ccap-eligibility-faqs---general-information-for-households-final.pdf?sfvrsn=4

————, "Program Changes Enable More Working Families to Access Child Care Assistance," February 16, 2017s. As of May 14, 2018:
https://www.louisianabelieves.com/newsroom/news-releases/2017/02/16/program-changes-enable-more-working-families-to-access-child-care-assistance

Louisiana Department of Revenue, "School Readiness Tax Credit," webpage, undated. As of April 30, 2018:
http://revenue.louisiana.gov/IndividualIncomeTax/SchoolReadinessTaxCredit

Louisiana Office of Student Financial Assistance, "Taylor Opportunity Program for Students (TOPS) Index Page," webpage, undated-a. As of November 6, 2017:
https://www.osfa.la.gov/schgrt6.htm

————, "The TOPS Performance Award," webpage, undated-b. As of December 21, 2017:
https://www.osfa.la.gov/tops_performance.html

Louisiana School Finder, website, undated. As of May 3, 2018:
http://www.louisianaschools.com/

Louisiana State Legislature, Early Childhood Care and Education Act, Acts 2012, No. 3, April 18, 2012. As of May 4, 2018:
https://legis.la.gov/Legis/Law.aspx?d=814864

Louisiana State University, "Freshman Admission Requirements," webpage, 2017. As of November 14, 2017:
https://sites01.lsu.edu/wp/admissions/become-a-tiger-2/freshmen/freshman-admission-requirements/

————, "Jump Start Pre-Engineering Career Pathway to Provide High School Students with Advanced Skills, College Credit," webpage, 2017b. As of November 14, 2017:
http://www.lsu.edu/eng/news/2017/06/2017-06-20-jump-start-pre-engineering-career-pathway.php

LSU—See Louisiana State University.

McDonnell, Lorraine M., and Richard F. Elmore, "Getting the Job Done: Alternative Policy Instruments," Educational Evaluation and Policy Analysis, Vol. 9, No. 2, 1987, pp. 133–152.

McDonnell, Lorraine M., and Milbrey W. McLaughlin, Education Policy and the Role of the States, Santa Monica, Calif.: RAND Corporation, R-2755-NIE, 1982. As of April 30, 2018:
https://www.rand.org/pubs/reports/R2755.html

McGuinn, Patrick, "Stimulating Reform: Race to the Top, Competitive Grants, and the Obama Education Agenda," Educational Policy, Vol. 26, No. 1, 2012, pp. 136–159.

National Council on Teacher Quality, *2017 State Teacher Policy Yearbook: National Summary*, Washington, D.C., 2017. As of January 24, 2018:
https://www.nctq.org/dmsView/NCTQ_2017_State_Teacher_Policy_Yearbook

National Institute for Early Education Research, *P–12 Alignment: Collaboration and Communication in Louisiana*, New Brunswick, N.J, 2015. As of November 14, 2017:
http://nieer.org/2015/06/24/p-12-alignment-collaboration-and-communication-in-louisiana

National Skills Coalition, *Middle-Skill Jobs State by State: Louisiana*, Washington, D.C., 2015. As of November 14, 2017:
https://m.nationalskillscoalition.org/resources/publications/2017-middle-skills-fact-sheets/file/Louisiana-MiddleSkills.pdf

The Nation's Report Card, "Data Tools," webpage, undated-a. As of November 13, 2017:
https://www.nationsreportcard.gov/data_tools.aspx

———, "Data Tools: State Profiles," Washington, D.C.: The Nation's Report Card, undated-b. As of April 13, 2018:
https://www.nationsreportcard.gov/profiles/stateprofile

NCTQ—*See* National Council on Teacher Quality.

Next Generation Science Standards, "Next Generation Science Standards: For States, by States," Washington, D.C.: Achieve, undated. As of November 14, 2017:
https://www.nextgenscience.org

Nobles, Wilborn P., "Louisiana ACT Scores Continue to Show Slow Progress in 2017," *The Times-Picayune*, August 9, 2017. As of December 19, 2017:
http://www.nola.com/education/index.ssf/2017/08/louisiana_2017_act_scores.html

Norton, Jill, Jennifer Ash, and Sarah Ballinger, *Common Core Revisions: What Are States Really Changing?* Abt Associates, 2017. As of November 15, 2017:
http://abtassociates.com/Perspectives/January-2017/Common-Core-Revisions-What-Are-States-Really-Chang

O'Donoghue, Julia, "Louisiana Senate Committee Funds TOPS, Reduces Mental Health Funding in State Budget," *NOLA.com*, 2017. As of November 6, 2017:
http://www.nola.com/politics/index.ssf/2017/06/louisiana_budget_tops.html

Phenicie, Carolyn, "Exclusive: Independent Review of ESSA Plans Rates States Strong on Accountability, Weak on Counting All Kids," *The 74*, June 26, 2017. As of November 13, 2017:
https://www.the74million.org/article/exclusive-independent-review-of-essa-plans-rates-states-strong-on-accountability-weak-on-counting-all-kids/

Pianta, Robert C., Karen M. La Paro, and Bridget K. Hamre, *Classroom Assessment Scoring System (CLASS) Manual, Pre-K*, Baltimore, Md.: Paul H. Brookes Publishing Company, 2008.

Regional Educational Laboratory Southwest at SEDL, "Leading the Way: How States Are Addressing Early Learning Under ESSA," 2017. As of November 14, 2017:
http://relsouthwest.sedl.org/bridge_events/2017-03-21_ece-essa/index.html

Robelen, Erik W., "Louisiana's 'Course Choice' Program Gets Underway," *Education Week*, Vol. 33, No. 2, August 27, 2013, p. 22.

Sabol, Terri. J., S. L. Soliday Hong, Robert C. Pianta, and Margaret R. Burchinal, "Can Rating Pre-K Programs Predict Children's Learning?" *Science*, Vol. 341, No. 6148, August 23, 2013, pp. 845–846.

Seashore Louis, Karen, Emanda Thomas, Molly F. Gordon, and Karen S. Febey, "State Leadership for School Improvement: An Analysis of Three States," *Educational Administration Quarterly*, Vol. 44, No. 4, 2008, pp. 562–592.

Sentell, Will, "Final Bill Approved in Common Core Agreement Designed to Address Concerns of Exam Opponents," *The Advocate*, June 12, 2015. As of November 13, 2017:
http://www.theadvocate.com/baton_rouge/news/education/article_053b99a3-f79b-5b47-b59c-c771c5b51067.html

Shapiro, Doug, Afet Dundar, Phoebe Khasiala Wakhungu, Xin Yuan, Angel Nathan, and Youngsik Hwang, *Signature Report 12 State Supplement: Completing College: A State-Level View of Student Attainment Rates*, Herndon, Va.: National Student Clearinghouse Research Center, 2017. As of November 14, 2017:
https://nscresearchcenter.org/signaturereport12-statesupplement/

Task Force on Textbooks and Instructional Materials, *Response to Act 389 of the 2015 Regular Session (R.S. 17:8.3)*, report to the House and Senate Committees on Education of the Louisiana Legislature, undated.

Taylor Plan, "Louisiana TOPS," New Orleans, La., undated. As of December 21, 2017:
http://www.taylorplan.com/resources/louisiana-tops/

University of Louisiana, "In-State Freshman Guaranteed Admission Criteria," 2017. As of November 14, 2017:
https://www.louisiana.edu/admissions/first-time-freshmen/requirements/guaranteed-admission

University of New Orleans, "In-State Freshmen Requirements," webpage, 2017. As of November 14, 2017:
http://new.uno.edu/admissions/apply-freshman/requirements

U.S. Census Bureau, "American Community Survey: Ranking Tables," webpage, undated. As of November 6, 2017:
https://www.census.gov/acs/www/data/data-tables-and-tools/ranking-tables/

Vitiello, Virginia E., Daphna Bassok, Bridget K. Hamre, Daniel Player, and Amanda P. Williford, *Measuring the Quality of Teacher-Child Interactions at Scale: The Implications of Using Local Practitioners to Conduct Classroom Observations*, Charlottesville, Pa.: University of Virginia, EdPolicyWorks Working Paper Series No. 52, November 2016. As of November 14, 2017:
https://curry.virginia.edu/uploads/resourceLibrary/52_Observing_Classroom_Interactions_At_Scale.pdf

WAFB, "TOPS Payments Stopped Immediately Due to State Budget Crisis," Baton Rouge, La., 2016. As of November 6, 2017:
http://www.wafb.com/story/31202290/
tops-payments-stopped-immediately-due-to-state-budget-crisis

Westendorf, Eric, "Curriculum, Defaults, and Equity," post to "Next Gen Learning in Action" blog at *Education Week* website, October 18, 2017. As of November 14, 2017:
http://blogs.edweek.org/edweek/next_gen_learning/2017/10/curriculum_defaults_and_equity.html

Will, Madeline, "Teacher-Made Lessons Make Inroads," *Education Week*, March 28, 2017. As of November 14, 2017:
https://www.edweek.org/ew/articles/2017/03/29/teacher-made-lessons-make-inroads.html